From the Somme to Singapore

Contemporary cartoon by George Sprod

From the Somme to Singapore

to Singapore

A Medical Officer
in Two World Wars

CHARLES HUXTABLE

Kangaroo Press

Dedicated to those who did not return.

Acknowledgments

I very much appreciate the help given to me by Colonel A.W. Sheppard, MC, who edited this book so carefully and took so much interest in its production.

I would like to thank the following people for helping me produce these memoirs: '

Hank Nelson, Wally Noonan, James Murray, Alec Bolton, Peter Wright, Beatrice Davis, Paddy Elworthy, Virginia Robinson and those Who gave photographs. Thanks to George Sprod for permission to reproduce his sketches.

Barbara Huxtable

Reprinted in paperback 1995
First published in 1987 by Kangaroo Press Pty Ltd
3 Whitehall Road Kenthurst NSW 2156 Australia
P.O. Box 6125 Dural Delivery Centre NSW 2158
Printed by Australian Print Group Maryborough 3465

ISBN 0 86417 745 3

Contents

Dr Charles Huxtable

Introduction

Charles Huxtable was born in Sydney on 30 September 1891, the son of Dr Louis Huxtable of College Street, and died on 29 July 1980. He was educated at 'Shore' and resided at St Paul's College whilst studying medicine. At the end of his course in 1914 he was recruited into the British Army as one of 'Kitchener's Hundred' and was posted to the Lancashire Fusiliers as a medical officer. During that war he was twice decorated for bravery in rescuing the wounded under heavy fire and with complete disregard for his own safety.

When the AIF arrived in Europe Dr Huxtable wanted to join them but red tape made this impossible for some time. The authorities, however, eventually came to their senses and he was to join the AIF in 1918 and remain with them until the Armistice.

After the war Dr Huxtable served at Sydney's Coast Hospital (now Prince of Wales), went to Scotland to obtain a Fellowship in surgery, then returned to Australia to practise in Southport, Queensland. He married Barbara Rowan in 1928 and had four children, the twins, Elizabeth and Barbie, and the sons, Bernard and Clive. On the outbreak of World War II he managed to join the 113 AGH, despite his being 48 years old, and was given a rank lower than that to which his previous war service entitled him. After only five months in Singapore he became a prisoner of the Japanese.

During his three and a half years of imprisonment Charles Huxtable worked tirelessly in the Australian and British hospitals and set a fine example to his fellow captives, being noted for giving up his own meagre rations to help his patients. For the greater part of his period of captivity Dr Huxtable was also able to keep a secret diary which reveals a great deal about the character of the man and the circumstances in which he found himself.

In his account of the Fall of Singapore and the reasons he saw for that defeat he displays a level and style of patriotism and Christian faith that he felt had passed a younger generation by. But even as he criticises 'that soul-destroying, lethargic, prudent, safety-first philosophy of the 1930s' he makes it equally clear that he was not a man to stand on dignity or to pull rank.

An 'unknown captain', he pays General Heath an unofficial call since 'we were all POWs together'. In another entry he is critical of the privilege and glamour that still attach to army rank even though 'fundamentally, we are all in the same bag'. In perhaps the most moving passages in the diaries, he farewells prisoners being taken off to work on the Burma railway without the postwar reader's knowledge of what such work was to entail. To the participant in history, the terrible details of the construction of the Bangkok to Moulmein railway are revealed only slowly and painfully.

As for prison life on Singapore Island, the cartoonist George Sprod, who was also there, lists ennui as one of the main enemies. The camp concerts and revues that were staged with a high degree of professionalism are by now well documented.

Charles Huxtable's diaries, however, describe an even greater range of activities and entertainments. After arduous and frequently distressing periods in woefully undersupplied hospitals, Huxtable attended medical seminars, a wide range of lectures including one on polo, and a number of classical concerts at some of which no fewer than three students of London's Royal Academy of Music performed. And what must any Japanese captors who recognised the music have made of the YMCA men playing the troops records of *Madam Butterfly?*

For a medical officer in Singapore, however, the period of captivity was distinguished by very much more than noble sentiment, seminars or fragmentary entertainments. Victims of appalling wounds, epidemics, cruel mistreatment and malnutrition had to be treated in makeshift hospital wards with inadequate equipment and few drugs. In an obituary notice for Dr Huxtable, Cotter Harvey, fellow doctor and prisoner, noted:

'Only those who have never been hungry will be surprised at the frequency of reference to food in the diary. Keeping alive on inadequate rations, with insufficient vitamins, was the constant struggle.

'Although as medical officers he and his friends and colleagues had more challenges to keep them mentally active and nearer to physical fitness, and were able to enjoy the stimulus of lectures and seminars, the finding, growing or purchase by any means of food, was the most important and constant theme of their lives.'

Charles Huxtable returned to Australia in September 1945. He was found to have tuberculosis and spent some months in hospital before resuming medical practice. Joining the Royal Flying Doctor service at Broken Hill he founded the Bush Children's Hostel Association. After Broken Hill he went to the Kimberly area as a Flying Doctor, then to the Eastern Highlands of New Guinea.

A hard-working doctor with a deep sense of duty, he was also keenly interested in world affairs. His account of his service in World War I, dictated at the age of 85 and rich in detail and sympathy for the victims of 'so much bungling', reveals the remarkable powers of recall and of

conviction that characterised Charles Huxtable's life dedicated to service
to others.

A.W. Sheppard

To Dr. Huxtable,

I remember you very well
You saved my Life in
Kranji Camp

Joe Hackett.

Major J.W.C. Wyett A.M.

Foreword

Like most combatant officers, I have always had a high regard for those distinguished enough in the army to be awarded a Military Cross. For a non-combatant to have earned one is rare indeed, and to be awarded a second one is almost unheard of. Yet that was the case with Charles — that most remarkable man — Captain Charles Huxtable, MC & bar.

Charles was a doctor of great skill and ability, yet his interests ranged beyond the realms of medicine and embraced anything which concerned or affected the welfare of his fellow men. As the awards I have quoted testify so well, he was absolutely fearless in the pursuit of these ideals, and for all the mildness and gentleness of his manner he was nevertheless both fearless and outspoken in the defence of his principles and not in any way afraid of attracting the displeasure of any established authority which allowed or condoned any practice which he saw to be wrong.

Leaving everything behind to volunteer for two world wars, Charles not only received extraordinary awards for valour in one, but also in the other he earned more decorations which would have been awarded him if the deeds of the men of the 8th Australian Division had received the recognition they so justly deserved.

Although extremely ill when he returned home, he soon took up the just fight again in civilian life with the Royal Flying Doctor Service, his unstinting work for a hospital in New Guinea and similar activities. In addition to such work at home, Charles was also decorated by a grateful Rhodesian government for his activities in striving so hard to prevent the suffering, injustice and hardship which he saw were imminent in that country.

If this book can give the reader some inspiration from an insight into the character of so outstanding a man, it will have more than repaid the efforts of those who have worked so well to bring it to us.

J.W.C. Wyett
Major, General Staff
8th Australian Division

Dr Huxtable with his wife, daughter and grandson, England 1979

Preface

Dr Charles Huxtable returned safely to Australia in September 1945, and after some months in hospital, resumed medical practice. He remained keenly interested in world affairs until his death on 29 July 1980.

This diary came home from Singapore with Dr Huxtable and was written in flimsy exercise books and on scraps of paper.

The diary was labelled 'Private' and, for that reason, I have deleted all personal messages and expressions of feeling, because I do not think he meant them for the eyes of readers other than members of his own family.

The World War I section was put together from a series of tapes made by my son, Professor Clive Huxtable. He used to sit with his father on Sunday evenings and question him about the war. Nearly all of the information came almost without notes of any kind and, though Dr Huxtable was eighty seven years old at that time, he remembered dates and places in a most remarkable way.

Barbara Huxtable

Mrs Charles Huxtable, December 1985

Captain Charles Huxtable while serving with the 2nd Battalion, Lancashire Fusiliers

PART ONE

The War to End All Wars, 1914-18

Battle of Arras
The wounded had reason to be deeply grateful to the Battalion's medical officer, Captain C.R. Huxtable, who showed the utmost bravery in attending to and evacuating them. At one stage seven of his stretcher bearers were buried by the explosion of a shell: he at once organized a party and dug them out, though shells continued to fall around.

Cambrai
The medical officer, Captain C.R. Huxtable MC, had once more shown a complete disregard of his personal safety in the discharge of his duties and he was awarded a bar to his decoration.

Major-General J.C. Latter, *History of the Lancashire Fusiliers*, Vol 1

In 1976, at the age of 85, Dr Huxtable dictated onto tape these memoirs of World War I to his son, Clive.

At the end of 1914 we were sitting for our final medical exams when Sir Thomas Anderson Stuart, the Dean, announced that he had received a cable from the War Office. The War had begun, of course, and we were all feeling a little unsettled.

The Dean made the announcement that the War Office had cabled him and the Dean of the Faculty of Medicine in Melbourne to the effect that 100 medical men were wanted for front-line work. Sir Thomas said, 'I think at least forty should come from Sydney'. The announcement was made during a gynaecological examination in the Great Hall of Sydney University, and it was rather difficult to concentrate on the subject after this. Those of us who were free to go answered the call of the War Office. Still others volunteered to go to New Guinea. The 40 volunteers were destined to go to France or Britain. To be perfectly honest, we had rather hoped that our action in volunteering for the British war effort might contribute to our success in our finals!

We had no idea to which regiment we would be attached. We simply fronted up to Victoria Barracks, signed on the dotted line and into the RAMC with the advice that we would be leaving shortly. I received my exam results in March 1915 and was on the water in the P & O passenger ship *Mawlwa* on 7 April, travelling as a civilian (although we were being paid one pound a day for the duration of the trip).

Once in the Mediterranean we were in the danger area and a gun was put aboard at Malta. However, our first incident connected with the war was at Suez when we entered the Canal in the evening and had to tie up to allow another ship travelling from the north to pass us. The Suez Canal is a very eerie, romantic place at night with the stillness of the desert surrounding us and the blackness pierced by the great, silent searchlight of the approaching ship. We were 50 to 60 yards from shore and, in the dusk of 24 April 1915, British troops on duty on the Canal gathered as close as they could to us, one yelling out to us in a broad Cockney accent: 'What's the news of the Dardanelles?' There was no radio in those days, so we had no way of knowing in advance of the momentous event that was to take place the following day at Gallipoli.

I think it must have been 25 April when we entered the Canal. In any event, after a time the fellows on shore were shouting messages to us when, as we were throwing tins of cigarettes to them (many of which fell in the water), the gong for dinner was heard along the decks. One or two of the men later emerged on deck in evening dress, to which those on shore responded: 'I'll have clear soup,' and 'Shame,' etc.! Oblivious to these insults, we went below to an excellent dinner, then proceeded through the Canal to Port Said. The following day we entered the Mediterranean, where all lights had to be extinguished at night, and in a day or two we reached Malta.

We were anxious to hear news of the Dardanelles campaign in Malta. In Port Said, of course, we heard of the landing and various wild rumours — that the Australians had broken through and were about to reach Constantinople.

Malta was full of hospitals. I discovered one which contained only British soldiers, so only gleaned very vague ideas of what had happened. However, one thing was sure: there had been heavy casualties. We went back to the ship for lunch prior to heading for the open sea again, and I'll never forget Lawrence Godfrey Smith's* excitement and enthusiasm. He had located a hospital which 'housed' Australians, had spoken to many of them and so was in a position to let us know, in graphic detail, of the beach landings.

We then had a four-inch gun screwed on to the poop, and a couple of marines used occasionally to practise target firing at a tub which they threw overboard. The effect on the passengers, when this practice took

*A famous pianist and teacher of pianoforte at Sydney Conservatorium. He fought as a gunner in France.

place, can be imagined. On reaching Marseilles, we heard of the sinking of the *Lusitania*. There was consternation amongst some of the passengers, who wanted to disembark and travel overland for the remainder of the journey to Britain. The ship's Captain, shrewd seaman that he was, advised against disembarkation, saying that it could be most dangerous as the Germans had in all probability mined the French railways. This ploy succeeded in stemming the rush and we continued our voyage to London without further incident.

On arrival, we had to report the next day to the War Office. I was staying with my aunt, whose flat became my headquarters for the duration of the war. She also had, I think, 20 New Zealand cousins and nephews who had enlisted, and they all were invited by her to make her flat their headquarters too. How she housed all our effects into that little flat, I will never know. I had stayed with her on my first trip to London in 1909, and she remained a wonderful little lady, bright, cheerful and optimistic.

I was eventually detailed for Devonshire (Totnes), but a particular friend, Jack Morlet, was detailed to Eastbourne. He prevailed on me to go and see the RAMC Colonel at the War Office requesting a change to Eastbourne, not in so many words of course. I had to take my courage in both hands when I came face to face with an enormous, stern colonel. When I explained that I had a special friend detailed for Eastbourne, he kindly said he 'would see what could be arranged'. So Eastbourne it eventually was!

London was filled with optimism and cheerfulness in spite of the anxieties of the retreat from Mons. When we arrived, news from the Front was hopeful: the German advance had been slowed after battles at Ypres and the Marne. People were optimistic that it would not be too long before the end of the war. However, Lord Kitchener told the nation that it would last three years and even that was an underestimation. The general feeling was, though, that hostilities would be over before Christmas 1915.

We spent three months at Eastbourne, first in lovely summer weather on the Sussex Downs. Ours, at that time, was a very pleasant war but we were impatient, as youngsters often are, to be through with our training and on our way to the Front. We were apprehensive that it would all be over before we had had an opportunity to play our part.

During the three months we were supposed to be in training I felt great sympathy for the unfortunate British sergeant majors who were detailed to train us. We were not the easiest types to train or discipline due, in part, to being medicos and of varying ages. A middle-aged Canadian remarked, 'Oh shucks, I'm not going to have this rubbish,' and walked out of the room. There was nothing the sergeant major could say but 'Please, Sir, come back'. Theirs was certainly an unenviable job; however, most of us tried to conform, doing physical jerks in the morning followed by ambulance drill, and then giving first-aid lectures to the stretcher-bearers. The training we particularly enjoyed was day-long route marches over the Sussex Downs. These really were lovely.

Every day or so, the bugle would blow, officers assemble, and march off to the CO's Headquarters. Once there, he would read out, 'The following officers will proceed to the Mediterranean' or 'the Middle East' or 'France' and we anxiously waited for our names to be called. After three months, our names appeared on the lists, Jack to Salonika and me to France. Notification of our postings was followed by details from the Orderly Room as to which trains to catch, etc. I was attached to the 7th Field Ambulance, and the whole unit was detailed to go to France.

We proceeded by train to Aldershot where we had a fortnight being fitted out, which included our own horse! Each officer was permitted a horse and we had great fun selecting our own. Several officers had never been on a horse before, so they were in for a few unpleasant surprises such as hitting the dust. I was familiar with riding, so Aldershot proved most enjoyable.

At the end of the fortnight we proceeded by train to Southampton, bound for Le Havre. The troopships travelled at night to lessen the risk of being torpedoed, and the whole unit was packed in like sardines in a can. Our arrival at Le Havre, a most miserable place, was in the early hours of the morning. It was raining and the base camps were absolutely horrible, bell tents in a sea of mud. Fortunately, it was only a transit camp and within two days we had moved on to a very pleasant country area, near Yvetot, further north. We trained there, living in billets among the French farms, and were involved in field exercises to keep the men out of mischief. After a month we received our marching orders to go to the Front, travelling by night but not knowing what was in store for us.

We were now part of Kitchener's new armies.

We left Yvetot, at the start of our long march, in September 1915. The first night we travelled 25 miles, the second night 20 miles, and the third and fourth in two lots of ten. It was very bad staff work to start men off on the longest section of the journey on the first night, with its resultant sore feet and blisters. It was all rather a painful business but, of course, during the day we rested, out of sight, in orchards, farmhouses and haystacks. Then when night came we moved painfully on.

During a brief stop on the third night I tied my horse up and went to sleep with my back propped against a tree. I remember waking and hearing what I thought was a thunder storm — a distant rumbling — but it was too constant and regular, never abating. This was the first time I heard the guns. We must have been still 20 miles from the front.

My most prevalent feeling at this time was that of sleepiness. Arriving at the front, we reached a town called Béthune late on the night of 24 September. It was the start of the terrible battle of Loos, supposedly the British breakthrough, under Sir John French, to convince the French that we were contributing wholeheartedly to the war effort. However, little advantage was gained by it, except that Britain had bogged down a large number of German troops. The losses were considerable —

approximately 60,000 men (included in this number was Rudyard Kipling's son).

The Field Ambulance Corps was dispersed in some large houses in Bethune. In the early hours of the morning, 25 September, the battle of Loos began. In spite of the bombardment I remember sleeping very well under a billiard table — we were draped all around the house, wherever there was room. The next morning we moved forward along the road as our troops had advanced with the initial attack. Then came my first experience of war, seeing the never-ending procession of walking wounded stretching as far as the eye could see.

It was a desperately sad sight, and I found it more so at night when we went out on to the battlefield in squads with stretcher parties to pick up any wounded we could find. It also gave us pride to think of the extraordinary courage of the fellows who had gone over 'the top'. Our infantry had had a bad time because they were exhausted when they went into the attack after the night marches of 50-odd miles.

Three Divisional generals were killed that day at Loos in the first attack, which discounts those rumours which were spread about — that the generals were never anywhere near the front. (One of them was General Thesiger, brother of the former Governor of Queensland and N.S.W., Lord Chelmsford).

For us, that particular battle lasted Saturday, Sunday and Monday. We had an ambulance dressing station in a ruined house in a village called Vermelles — about ten miles in front of Béthune where the communication trenches, leading up to the line, commenced. The country there at Loos is flat and black with views of the great slag heaps of the mines in the distance. We had a Red Cross flag flying and people were dropping in, or being carried in, all day long for their wounds to be dressed. At night an officer would take a couple of parties of stretcher-bearers along the communication trench and then out on top on to a road. We had maps of the area with map readings so that we could pick up wounded between, say, Point A and B, and take them back along the road to the waiting ambulances, a distance of about a mile or two. The front-line trenches were not far in front of Vermelles, or rather what had been the front line as the Germans had been pushed back a couple of miles. That first night we were collecting not only our own Divisional members but also those from the Highland Division as there had been much confusion in the attack. I can still see in my mind's eye the terrible losses sustained by the Highlanders — bodies lying about everywhere just as they had fallen.

Loos was very much a battle of rifles and heavy artillery which contrasted with later stages of the war when there were mainly machine-guns, apart from snipers. But Loos was a constant crackle of rifle fire all over the whole arc of the offensive area. Stray bullets were whizzing about in all directions, but you had to be very unlucky to be hit by one of them.

For guns, we had a lot of 60-pounder batteries, and one was just behind our cottage. They were firing in salvos. A lone 60-pounder makes an ear-splitting blast on its own but four of them firing at once not only shook the earth but also dislodged a few more tiles from our roof. The rifle and gunfire were unending as also were the flares of various colours and descriptions — all most impressive if one could forget, momentarily at least, the tremendous toll of human life and limb.

A friend of mine, Lieutenant Harold Woodford of the 8th Berkshires, went over the top on 8 October, a fortnight after the battle began. It was a month later before his body was discovered and retrieved, a most tragic thing for his mother in England. However, it demonstrates how very difficult it was to recover all the dead.

In the book *From Mons to Ypres* written by the American, Colman, which I read long after the war, the story is told of the Grenfell twins who were wonderful examples of British professional officers. Julian Grenfell (1888-1915) wrote the magnificent poem 'Into Battle' in which he described:

> In dreary doubtful waiting hours,
>   Before the brazen frenzy starts,
> The horses show him nobler powers;
>   O patient eyes, courageous hearts!

After this battle, I went north to the Ypres salient still with the 74th Field Ambulance. There were about eight medical officers in the Field Ambulance, and one of the other officers and I were lucky to have a comfortable dugout. Sometimes, as at the battle of Loos, we were desperately overworked but, at the other times with peaceful trench warfare, we were not nearly busy enough.

When all was quiet on the Ypres front, I found it interesting to go for a walk through the ruins salvaging souvenirs from the great pile of rubble that had been the Cathedral and where part of the famous old Cloth Hall was still standing. Some fellows went too far in their eagerness to souvenir: one took down the sign of the Ypres Railway Station and somehow managed to spirit it back to England.

After a while I was transferred from the Field Ambulance and was attached to the 9th Royal Sussex Regiment. In order to get to the battalion, my good batman, John Dix, and I had a long walk one night, up through Ypres, down through the Lille Gate and out on to a desolate road for a couple of miles until we reached a long, winding communication trench. This took us up to Maple Copse under the shelter of Hill 60. I lived in a dugout in Maple Copse (named by the Canadians), among the stumps of pine trees, with a rather grim, war-weary colonel. From our shelter we used to go on a long tour through Sanctuary Wood. Where the trenches were low, signs had been erected: 'Snipers. Keep down', but being a bit careless on one occasion as I walked past I narrowly missed being struck by a bullet which flicked up the snow just behind me. Needless to say, I paid greater respect to such notices in future.

I was welcomed in the dugout by the captain of the company, by the name of McNair. I had the greatest admiration for these young British officers in the frontline regiments. The 9th Battalion was one of the wartime battalions, not one of the regulars, and they made a cult of cheerfulness. They never talked of their scars, or wounds, or losses. They lived in, and for, the present, and when you analyse it, that was the wisest course in those days.

My dressing station was in a ruined house in the village. Battalion Headquarters were, I suppose, 200 yards away in a trench dugout but I lived in the heap of ruins to tend the wounded when they were brought in at night. Occasionally I had to go to the front line in daytime if there had been an attack. The Germans at this time were using a lot of minnenwurfers, ghastly weapons which resembled great torpedoes. If they landed away from a trench there was no harm done. However, if one landed in a trench, I was urgently needed.

On one of the walls of the house there were some decorations by Captain Bruce Bairnsfather — the Warwicks had evidently lived in the same building in this village.

The Scout Officer, young Lieutenant Castle, had found special favour in the eyes of the war-weary colonel, perhaps because he used to cheer him up. Castle used to delight in going out at night and crawling over to the German trenches and, in his report one day, he mentioned that he had heard a German band playing. The colonel reprimanded him for being frivolous in his reporting. The young officer insisted he had heard the band, and when pressed to say what had been played, he replied: 'As far as I could make out, Sir, it was playing the "Hymn of Hate" ', a hymn that the Germans had recently composed.

One morning we heard that Captain McNair had been awarded a VC for some heroic deed a couple of months earlier. I remember the good fellowship there was, everyone rushing across to congratulate him. He was still in bed, and all he could say was, 'Oh, shut up you fools, get out of the place; I want to get some sleep'. He was under the impression that they were pulling his leg. But it was the truth, and when I visited Britain last time, I went into the Cathedral in Chichester and there, on the Royal Sussex Regimental Memorial, I scanned the names and there was his — Captain McNair, VC.

In April I went on leave to London. I tried to join the AIF, then back from Egypt and Gallipoli. Gallipoli had been evacuated at the end of 1915 and by April 1916 the troops were filtering over to France and the AIF headquarters were at Horseferry Road. After reporting back after two days, I was informed that the only way to join the AIF was to return to Australia and join up there. To me this was ridiculous so I rejoined the RAMC.

London, at the time, was crowded with troops. Everywhere khaki and cheerfulness. Those at home had no idea of what it was like at the front. The Somme and the U-boat era, with the sinking of 40 ships a week, were yet to come.

I was eventually sent from London to Boulogne to join the 13th Stationary Hospital on the hill outside the town. This hospital was crowded with wounded coming in convoys from the front.

Just as a point of interest, every wounded man was given a tetanus anti-toxin and typhoid vaccine, and of all the hundreds and thousands of wounded men (I alone would have seen thousands in hospitals and would treat many not-so-seriously wounded), I never saw a case of either. There appeared to be no serum sickness, apart from cases of an irritating rash ten days after being administered. Of course, if there had been a typhoid outbreak, then the potential would have been there for the whole army to be wiped out, as the sanitation in northern France was lamentable.

At the hospital there was a Dr Nutall of Birmingham, an excellent surgeon. It was not unusual to learn of a train full of wounded arriving, usually at night, and the ambulances would be at the hospital within half an hour. The admissions on each occasion could be at least 100 to 200 men, and I remember Dr Nutall saying to me that many a man's chances of survival depended mainly upon the amount of time that you could give him. There was so much rush during these times that you could literally save a man or lose him. Blood transfusions were not, by any means, in common usage then. I was amazed the first time I saw the effect of a blood transfusion on a man: one moment he appeared to be at death's door, and ten minutes later he was sitting up asking for a cigarette. It is so much taken for granted now, but then, if it had been in wider use, so many more lives could have been saved.

From Boulogne I returned to the front line. I remember a scotty little sister at the hospital saying to me: 'A young man like you shouldn't be spending your time down here. You should be up at the front.' I felt offended, but only replied, 'Thank you, Sister, I probably will be before long'.

The attack on the Somme Valley, the largest yet organised by Britain in the war, opened on 1 July. The following day I was ordered up to the front, so took a train to Acheux on the Somme. Several medical officers had been wounded or killed that day and I had a two kilometre walk from Acheux to a village called Bertram Court where the 4th Divisional Headquarters were stationed. The 4th Division was a regular Division and I felt honoured to be placed with a regular. I was given the choice of joining the Warwickshires or the 2nd Lancashire Fusiliers. I didn't know much at that time about the Warwickshires, but was impressed by the Lancashire Fusiliers' exploits in the battle of Spion Kop in the South African War, so elected to join them. I stayed the night at Divisional Headquarters in a tent in an orchard and the next day was sent by ambulance to the Brigade Headquarters where I met Victor Hawkins who was at that time seconded to Brigade duties. (We have remained friends ever since.) Victor thought that the Lancashire Fusiliers were 'the best crowd in the Division'.

After lunch at Brigade Headquarters I had to foot it to the trenches, with a guide, for a couple of miles before entering the muddy communication trench. After about a mile along the latter, my guide and I came to the support trenches of the Lancashires. They had taken part in the attack on 1 July and when I joined them about the 5th they were still licking their wounds. They had suffered severely, and were to suffer a further ten days before being relieved.

The Battalion had actually attacked between Beaumont Hamel, to be seen on the hillside, and a place called Serres, up on the left. What struck me most was the cheerfulness of the troops — one was not permitted to be gloomy. There appeared to be optimism, however badly events were turning out, but of course they lived with grief as one by one their comrades were killed.

We were relieved on the 21 July at night, and there followed a ten-mile march back through Bertram Court to a hut camp where we stayed for a few days. We then marched to Dulonge, and from there caught the train to Caselle on the Belgian border. Our marching commenced again and we eventually reached Poperinghe. We were taken out of the Somme area but were back again in October (the Somme offensive continued through until November). We also had a spell again in the Ypres salient.

One incident in Poperinghe stands out in my mind. One night a Belgian peasant came to my billet and said 'Piccaninny, piccaninny, come quick'. I gathered it was a confinement case and rushed to the Dressing Station to get my medical case and my trusty first-aid man, McCarthy, a good Irishman unfortunately a little the worse for liquor. There was no one else to take his place, however, so we set off, with the Belgian as guide, to a house some distance away. There must have been 13 people standing round the bed, mostly old women, so I ordered them out of the room, and the windows to be opened. The air was stifling. Fortunately I had had experience with confinements at Crown Street so, with McCarthy a little more sober by then and clutching a lamp, the baby was delivered. It had been a breach case; however, the delivery was successful, and the baby was fine.

I didn't have long to become famous in Poperinghe as we left the town soon afterwards, en route to the trenches at Hill 60. During a rest period in my dugout the blankets parted and who should walk in but Stuart Hay, a Sydney friend. Stuart was an officer with the Field Artillery and until his appearance I was unaware that the Australians had arrived. He had come to explore this line and find the observation posts because they were taking over from us a few days later.

Our next stay was at Laverting Chateau, a lovely old chateau some way off the Ypres Road between Poperinghe and Ypres. It had never been shelled so it was presumed it belonged to people in Germany. I lived on the top floor and felt none too comfortable when the Germans started shelling just over its roof to a place beyond. We stayed there for two weeks, more or less in comfort. My hygiene corporal, Corporal Lomax, a man of about 49, was very keen on hygiene and had a very classy incinerator reserved for Headquarters' use. When I remonstrated that I did not think he should have used such good bricks for such a purpose he replied that he had taken them from the nearby bombed-out church — they were just lying around so he thought they should be put to good use!

On 15 September we were ordered south again after 12 days on the Ypres salient, this time travelling 70 miles south to Amiens. We reached the deserted, broad, empty streets of Amiens in the middle of the night, continuing for another ten miles, to Corbie on the Somme.

Corbie was a delightful little village and I lived in a billet with Willy Fanner and another fellow who came from Tierra del Fuego. Englishmen had come from all over the world to enlist and this fellow, Stephenson, was all of 40. I remember that we used to go up to a little stationery shop principally to yarn with a pretty girl called Toinette. She was a real little flirt and she preferred English officers because they were 'si grands et les soldats si petits'. This was true — the officers were tall and the Lancashire soldiers, on the whole, were stocky and short.

We left Corbie after 12 days, and after various marches, arrived at Albart. I remember that we went past the hanging figure that hung for years from the steeple of a church. The figure was that of the Virgin, handing upside down and a legend surrounded it — that when it fell, the war would be over. I could never understand why someone did not knock it down.

We finally reached the Somme fighting. One of my most vivid memories of the day we arrived at the front line was of a French battalion coming out and I shall never forget their haggard faces, pale and unshaven. However, we had arrived to do our stint and we had two horrible attacks — the first on the 12 October.

The French armies had been hard pressed for most of the year. The senseless episode of Verdun had commenced on 21 February and fierce fighting had raged until late June, after which it continued spasmodically until September 1916. At the insistence of the French Prime Minister, Briand, against the wishes of Joffre, and under the command of Pétain, the battle for Verdun went ahead, a bait specially prepared by the German general Falkenhayn to draw off French forces from the Western Front, thus leaving Britain on her own.

Verdun was saved, it has been said, by the automobile engine. Three thousand lorries passed and repassed every day along 'the sacred way', the only road of communication. Verdun was saved, too, at the cost of the French Army, for the bitter battle so shattered the French fighting spirit that it brought it to the verge of mutiny.

I understand that claims have often been made that the British offensive on the Somme was launched to divert German forces from Verdun. I find this hard to accept as the fierce Verdun fighting had all but ceased before the British offensive commenced. Be that as it may, we were supposed to hold the German forces further north. We were, therefore, thrown into the Somme battle on 12 October. Troop losses were enormous. Battalion Headquarters were in a sunken road about 100 yards behind the trenches, but it was overcrowded, so I had to find another area to treat the wounded. There were also steps down to HQ, so this was another reason to find an alternative dressing area.

I eventually settled upon another section in this sunken road — a German latrine trench just off the road. We filled in the latrine, and enlarged and widened the trench a bit so we could get stretcher cases away from the road. All in all, it was a grim, exhausting four days.

About the only thing the British did not lack was enthusiasm. They were a volunteer army for the most part (very few conscripts), had had only rudimentary training, barely knew how to shoot accurately, and had been taught to fight in a straight line formation — thus unable to operated as scattered units. The officers were also raw recruits who had been taught to expose themselves unnecessarily to enemy fire so that their losses were sometimes six times higher than that of other ranks.

Attempting to locate the wounded at the front and bring them to safety for treatment soon became a nightmare. The bombardments pitted the ground so heavily with shell craters that orderly movement over the battlefield was virtually impossible. By now the autumn rains were falling, turning the battlefield into a quagmire. A party of stretcher-bearers with a stretcher case could take up to four hours to get to the dressing station.

On 23 October the men of the battalion were thrown again into battle, and when this particular action was over, all our officers had been killed except the colonel, the adjutant, Captain Watkins, and myself. I think in each attack we lost at least 200 men. Our battalion ranks had thinned greatly, not more than a couple of hundred left. However, the ranks would soon be replenished with 1917 fast approaching.

I later had the opportunity of flying over the battlefield and it happened in the following way.

After our engagement, which had commenced on the 23rd we were moved back behind the lines for a rest. Our quarters were in a hut camp way back behind Trones, Burnefais and Delville Woods. An Irishman, Colonel Bourke, had been sent to command us and I remember, because of a loose cartilage in his knee, he used to carry a great staff to support him walking, especially in the mud.

During rest periods, when we were away from the trenches, we used to go riding for relaxation. On one occasion, Colonel Bourke suggested that I accompany him on a ride the following day to visit a nearby squadron where, he said, there were some Australians. I rode over with him and met the commander of No. 9 Squadron at Morlancourt, Victor Bell (who was later to become a relative by marriage). At lunchtime

Colonel Bourke asked Victor if any of the fellows were flying that afternoon, adding 'I'm sure the doctor would like a flight'. I could have killed him for the suggestion! However, I felt I couldn't demur, and when one of the young fellows, Johnny Hall, said he would be flying up to the lines to reconnoitre and would be happy to take me, there was nothing I could do but accept as graciously as was possible, considering how I was feeling.

Although terrified I was amused that, as we were flying over the lines, Johnny kept expressing his sympathy for those on the ground. I had the reverse sentiments.

It was a very flimsy plane — an open-air machine with me in front and Johnny behind. Johnny said, 'When we get over Lesboeuf, which I understand is the place where we will be holding the line, I'll rock the machine'. It seemed like hours later, but in reality only about ten minutes, the plane was rocking like a canoe. When I looked around, Johnny was pointing straight down. Apart from a few shell bursts, the land was complete desolation.

At that time on the Somme, our aircraft were playing a big part. They had superiority over the German craft and used to range far over the German lines. The Germans rarely reciprocated. One of my recollections of the Somme battles is that of seeing our aeroplanes flying low over the trenches with the German machine guns trained on them.

It was a nightmare landscape. However, when I went back four miles or so the memory of it was erased, in part, when I saw my horse waiting to take me the remaining five miles to the hut camp, where the good old quartermaster had hot tea ready. I was fortunate to have a tent to myself after the Somme battle at the end of October and I lay down on my bunk to read my mail at about four in the afternoon. The letters were still unread at four the following afternoon, I was quite exhausted, having not slept for the previous three days.

The last Somme attack came on 13 November. There had virtually been no headway in the bitter months of fighting. The front had advanced here and there about five miles. The French had lost nearly 200,000 troops, the British 420,000 and the Germans about 450,000. As Verdun had destroyed the spirit of the French Army, so the Somme destroyed the spirit of the British. The volunteers, no longer idealistic, had no faith in anything other than that of loyalty to their comrades. in the minds of the soldiers the war no longer had a purpose. The losses in the Somme battles were in the forefront of everyone's minds, we didn't talk about them but felt them all most deeply.

Late in October, when the Somme battles were almost over, a note of optimism crept in. General Nivelle, in local command in Verdun, made a surprise attack and regained virtually all the territory that had been lost in the first half of the year, with few casualties.

At one stage during the year I managed to get to Paris on leave. I remember that I particularly wished to have leave on a certain date, and was ably assisted to this end by a young staff officer at Divisional Headquarters, so that I could meet up with Bill Page, my old friend from Sydney University.

An amusing incident rather surprised me in these more restful days. I had always imagined that those in the lower ranks were most respectful to officers. But in the old regular battalions, rank ceased to exist on occasions and formalities were dispensed with. One evening, Major Blanko, 2i/c, was playing bridge when his batman came to tell him that his hot bath was ready. The baths had to be heated in tins out in the yard. The major replied that he would be there presently but that he just wanted to finish the game. This occurred three or four times before the Major said, 'Look here, thanks, but I think I won't have the bath tonight. It's a bit late.' The orderly drew himself up and said, 'Excuse me, Sir, you are going to have your bath if I have to sit up all night'. The Major went out immediately and had his hot bath.

I was delighted to learn from the CO that I was due for leave on 10 November and I went down the line with Sergeant Major Granger, a drummer sergeant, most skilful and a splendid fellow. With half a dozen other old veterans, we went over to Britain for the usual ten days.

Although it was such a different world in London, people appeared most appreciative of all that the men were going through at the front. It was after the war that it was 'business as usual' and those at home forgot the tremendous sacrifice of millions. The victory, if victory it could be called, was touch and go — we were saved at the eleventh hour by the entry of the Americans after the collapse of Russia.

Returning to the front after being on leave was always a depressing business. The luxury of hot baths and blankets was behind us. Ahead of us, on 20 November, was a Channel crossing, made dangerous by the lurking submarines, and a bitter winter leading us into 1917. Entry into France was through several ports including Le Havre and Calais. Southampton to Le Havre was believed to be a safer crossing than Dover to Calais. However, spending a night in the hut camp at Le Havre was depressing in the extreme. Once at Le Havre there followed a most boring experience: five days and five nights on the same train. We were searching for the battalion. None of the transport officers seemed to know where they were. We heard that they had left Malayville, the village near Abbeville, but no-one seemed to know where they were newly situated. Eventually we located them just as they were vacating camp to go to the front on 3 December. The battalion was to relieve a section of the line which, up to then, had been held by the French Army.

Winter had arrived, bitterly cold and wet. On our march forward to the front, my cockney groom, Skipper (who tended his horse and mine), and I got hopelessly lost in the dark. We had paused to place a sick man on my horse and continued on foot. Still lost at daybreak, we were given breakfast by an RFC Squadron and eventually linked up with the battalion at 10.00 a.m., just as they were leaving camp for another long march.

We could not have inherited a worse section of the line. The flat country was a sea of mud and there were none of what we called communication trenches. We had to walk up over the top along a cobblestone road which was full of holes, and as the men could only go up at night, they frequently got lost.

After locating the batalion dugout near the front line, I went back about a mile to establish a dressing station in a dugout in the side of the road where I spent the next four nights. We did two tours of duty of eight days each — four days in the front line and four days in the support trenches, about 800 yards behind the front-line trenches. Four days in the front line was just about all that the men could endure standing in mud all the time with virtually no sleep.

With the intense cold before Christmas the mud froze, making conditions a little easier.

At this time, there was very little activity. In fact the Germans came out on top towards Christmas and my friend, Jim Watkins, who was 2i/c at the time, told me that a German officer had come over to him and offered him a cigar. Because the Germans were walking about on top, our fellows followed suit. When news reached Headquarters a furious message came 'to stop fraternising at once, get back into the trenches and start firing'. Our men went back into the trenches and shouted to the Germans to get back also. Of course we didn't open fire on them — after all, there must be some honour, even in war.

I remember going along the line one night, to see if I could help to cheer the fellows up, when I came across a pair of boots protruding from a dugout. A sort of rabbit warren had been dug into the side of the dugout, allowing a man to crawl in up to his knees. At this particular spot, I noticed a crack had appeared in the mud which might have caused a cave-in. I woke the owner of the boots to point out the crack to him. 'Oh, I know that, Sir,' he replied, 'I've seen it. It'll be all right until morning.' And so it was.

Our time at Sailly-Sel was really the most miserable part of trench life we ever experienced. Going up to the front line at night, we were under fire from all sorts of German artillery. Many men lost their way and perished from the cold as they often got stuck in the mud, knee deep, and could not extricate themselves. One night some stretcher-bearers were trying to pull a man out of the mud. Being exhausted, the man lay back as the bearers were trying to extract one leg at a time. Apparently he fell asleep from exhaustion, but this proved too much for the stretcher-bearers who were also worn out from lack of sleep. One slapped the fellow's face saying, 'What do you think this is, some sort of game? Help your own bloody self.' Men were often so exhausted and dispirited that they did not particularly care what happened to them.

A young lieutenant from the Essex Regiment was brought to my dressing dugout one day and the moment I saw him I knew he would not live long. When I asked him for his name so that I could write it on his casualty ticket, he said calmly, 'My name is Tokley, T-O-K-L-E-Y', and not long after he died. I found this sang-froid very inspiring. This was one of many occasions when I wished I were able to give a blood transfusion.

We eventually left Sailly-Sel to go five miles further north to Sailly-Laurette. Our life there was very pleasant, plenty to eat and the men playing games in addition to their training. Also the cold and the frozen ground contributed to making life pleasant. It was the wet, slippery, sinking mud that was cursed.

At Sailly-Laurette I first met Brigadier Adrian Carton de Wiart, afterwards General de Wiart, who distinguished himself in the Second World War where we met again under strange circumstances.

An amusing incident happened here concerning the Roman Catholic padre, a good fellow by the name of Ryan. Short and stout, he decided to hold a church service for another unit at another village, Sailly-Sec. Padre Ryan asked to borrow my horse but I hedged, saying that, because she had not been ridden for a while, she might be too fresh and cause some trouble. 'I'll be right, Bones,' he said. 'Will you arrange for your groom to bring her up at ten, Sunday morning?'

At ten the Padre arrived, clutching two green canvas buckets full of books — hymnbooks I suppose — which were hung, one on either side of my little black mare. Skipper heaved the Padre into the saddle and off they went at a trot down this cobble-stoned road. The buckets started to bump the sides of the little mare and she quickened her pace, eventually breaking into a gallop, with sparks flying from the cobble stones. The padre came to a sticky end several hundred yards further on, crashing to the cobbles in a sea of hymn books! We rushed to help him up, but he didn't appear any the worse for his little adventure.

The horses also fared badly in the wintry rain and mud. The British Army had a bad habit of clipping them. The Transport Officer had my little mare clipped without my permission and the poor creature died of cold. Good horses were hard to come by. Eventually, I was given a horse by the name of Fritz, a German horse and a real veteran which had been with the battalion since the retreat from Mons. I remember one billet we were in when Skipper came round to see me and told me proudly that he had managed to obtain a stall for Fritz under a house in which some of the men were billetted. The following morning, I asked Skipper how Fritz had survived the night and the reply was, 'There's been a bit of a row, Sir. He was hollering like hell all night.'

Our time at Sailly-Sel bred a lot of 'trench feet' — swollen feet — which was the main reason why the men remained in the line for only four days. We also had a certain amount of 'trench fever', due to lice, but nothing too serious. My horses were used mainly to carry sick men and those with sore feet.

Some men were invalided out with psychiatric disturbances, but regulations were tough in those days. Sometimes I have pangs of remorse, but it doesn't do to dwell on past mistakes. If you relax and give favours to one man, there may be a flood of others. Being a medical officer had its problems. You couldn't be soft-hearted, yet at the same time you wanted to be fair. Before an attack on the Somme, an officer who had stuck a pencil in his eye came to me. The mark of an indelible pencil showed on the white of one eye and it certainly looked a bit sore. However, I didn't think it was nearly bad enough for him to miss the impending attack the next morning. He was killed in the attack. Incidents like this used to haunt me but you can only make the best judgement possible at the time.

On the other hand, the main characteristic of the Army was one of sustained cheerfulness which appeared genuine, not artificial. Although the Somme crushed the idealism, I still think there was an underlying faith that Britain would eventually triumph, however dark the clouds in 1916 or in 1917, which dawned in the midst of a bitter winter with little hope of victory. However, it was to be a momentous year with the exit of Russia and the entry of the United States.

From Sailly-Laurette, we went into training for the Battle of Arras — a lead-up to Vimy Ridge and to the offensive Third Battle of Ypres. The outskirts of Arras formed the front line.

About the time of the battle, we never knew what was coming, only that spring always meant some offensive. However our training continued in the countryside quite close to Arras. If we were not up at the line, the men would go on fatigue duties to the front, or carry rations to help other troops in the brigade, or take part in working parties preparing trenches and other such duties.

Colonel Griffin had joined us. An old regular, he was much beloved by the battalion, and when a CO is liked and trusted it is remarkable to feel the surge in morale in the whole unit.

We also had an orderly, John Carr, a real grim old Lancashire fellow who had been out since Mons and was a born optimist. I can hear him now telling the newcomers to keep their heads up — 'What are you ducking your heads for? Keep your heads up' — even when the shells were whistling overhead. Unfortunately, John had a fondness for rum, and whenever he was promoted to lance corporal, he didn't hold his stripes very long as he would take solace in the bottle and become private Carr again.

After a long night of waiting, we eventually got the order to march. We set off in the dark, and after a couple of hours there was a sudden blast of gunfire a few miles ahead of us. The barrage started in one instant. We kept on marching until daylight, when we found ourselves in a field near St Nicholas, north of Arras, where the great cookers were lit and we had breakfast.

This was the waiting area where our brigade was assembled. All around the ridge just in front of us were guns, wheel to wheel; there was a feeling of safety and confidence that you had when your own guns were firing.

Shortly before 9 a.m. we left the field as a solitary German aeroplane came over at great height. About a quarter of an hour later the German shells started landing in the middle of the field we had so recently vacated. The plane, of course, was a spotter for the German guns.

We had not been in the first attack, which had been at daybreak, but we followed up about mid-morning with the Duke of Wellington's and the King's Own Royal Lancs. The earlier attacks having been successful, we found it was just a matter of walking over the German front trenches which were like a sea of chalk — completely churned up. We wondered how many survived, and precious few had.

We felt elated at this success; it felt like the beginning of the end of the war, just walking straight ahead for five miles until we reached the village of Fampoux. The Scarpe River, which flows through Arras, was about half a mile away on our right.

Continuing through this undulating country we noticed very few German wounded lying around; the first attacking battalions must have evacuated them. We saw several groups of prisoners hurrying back. One particular crowd — about 30 in all — caught sight of me. I was walking on my own at the time, with a medical orderly, and I had a roll of splinting under my arm which must have looked like a machine-gun. They came rushing over to me with their hands up. Little did they know I didn't even have a revolver. Quite embarrassing. We just motioned to them to keep moving, to go back, which they did most willingly.

I remember coming across another German, a real Prussian, a proud man with a moustache, lying on his own with a compound fracture to his leg. I went over and signified to him that I was going to dress it and opened my bag and took out some cotton wool, splints and so on. He never said a word, never groaned with pain, but fixed such a baleful glare on me that I found it rather disturbing. For all I knew, he could have had a concealed weapon, but I didn't think to search him first. I only thought of his broken leg. After setting his leg as best I could and giving him a shot of morphia which I always carried on me to give injections, I left him there for someone else to pick up.

The next few days were spent at Fampoux. Two of our companies, including A Company, commanded by my friend Captain Willie Fanner, established a line along a crest, just north of the houses of the village. In Fampoux I set up a dressing station in the cellar of a house and placed the Red Cross flag outside so that the fellows would know where to come. Away south of the river was a great ridge of high ground on which I remember seeing the cavalry silhouetted against the sky as they moved in to attack a village, Monchy le Preux, opposite Fampoux on the south side of the Scarpe. It was heartbreaking seeing men and horses, one minute trotting along the skyline, the next falling before the shells.

On the second day for our second attack, the cavalry came up, a mistaken idea of course. They were so vulnerable as they stood for hours along the road trying to shelter under trees which were barely in leaf.

Most French roads are lined with poplars and other trees which afford little protection. Horses and riders eventually disappeared through the village at the time of our second push forward. This wonderful arm, the cavalry, suffered considerable losses and all to no avail. It didn't help the advance, which had become stalemated, and it was a foolish step on the part of the commanders to deploy the cavalry which, with the advent of tanks, had become out-dated.

The day after the attack eight ambulancemen were sent to me at Fampoux. The village had been fairly heavily shelled by us and was more or less in ruins, but the cellar seemed a reasonably safe dugout where a stretcher could be carried down the steps with some sort of shelter. I arranged for seven of the ambulancemen to stay in a cellar of a similar house directly across the road. The eighth I kept with me to act as liaison to summon the others when needed.

Sad to relate, during an attack later in the morning when shells were landing in the village, a high explosive shell struck the house and cellar opposite. I sent the eighth ambulanceman across the road to see how the others were faring and he returned, with a white face, to tell me the building was a pile of rubble. Two of the Lancashire men, the liaison ambulanceman and I worked for about half an hour moving bricks to retrieve the bodies. Although there was no barrage now, the occasional German shell fell in the village. Eventually we unearthed three of the men, quite dead. We started shouting, but there were no replies. It was all a desperately sad business. We couldn't unearth them under those tons of bricks. I couldn't delay any longer because the wounded were being brought to the dressing station for my attention. But the above episode was evidently the reason for my Military Cross.

At night I went to the front line to see Willy Fanner, and found him and his men in great heart. In the attack the morning before, he had got one of the men to kick a football over the trench, they were using the German trenches of course. In an attack two days later they made another advance, only a matter of 200 yards, but they never went much further than another mile in the Battle of Arras. We fought two costly futile attacks across low-lying land from Fampoux near some chemical works at Roeux. The Germans, however, had the benefit of large reinforcements and we could not dislodge them. It became the same old story — the offensive continued for too long in the same area.

The Battle of Arras had commenced just north of the Hindenburg Line (known to the Germans as the Siegfried Line) and we learned some time later of the magnificent attack by the Canadians on Vimy Ridge and of the fierce fighting to the south by the Australians at Bullecourt. Allenby's army had penetrated more than six miles in some places. But once again losses were horrendous: about 140,000 British and 100,000 German casualties.

Although tanks had been used in the Somme offensive since mid-September the previous year, I never saw any at Arras. Perhaps the reason was that where we were the ground was undulating and the river would have been an obstruction as tanks couldn't cross rivers in those days.

I was distressed one morning when Willy Fanner was brought into the dressing station on a stretcher with a bullet wound through both sides of his chest. He was a very conscientious man and if he couldn't get quickly from one part of the line to the other along his company, he'd simply get out on top. On this particular morning a sniper had caught him at dawn; it started snowing that day and when Willy reached me, he had pneumo thorax. I sealed him up with gauze packing in the dressing station and sent him off down the line, thinking that would be the last time I'd see him. He was operated on at the casualty clearing station further back, eventually recovered, and a year later was in France again.

It was at one of the attacks at the chemical works that I saw my only case of shell shock. It was an officer who had lost an eye in a bomb accident the previous November. Very gallantly, he volunteered to go up to the front again. He didn't need to prove anything, he was a brave man. However, it proved too much for him. Every time one of our guns went off, while I was guiding him to the support lines, he would fall to the ground trembling. He insisted on going on, but when I reached his company I spoke to his company commander and suggested that he be sent back to me as soon as possible. I could see he was determined to try, but he could only manage to stick it for a day or two. I sent him back down the line. Having lost an eye, he had lost his nerve with it, and small wonder, really.

Another incident worth recalling is that of a man who looked after the pigeons. Carrier pigeons were used when a big attack and advance were expected and a man trained to work with carrier pigeons was attached to Battalion Headquarters. After that first successful attack near Arras, when we were occupying the German trenches and digging them a bit deeper, I engaged the pigeon man in conversation. He was leaning against the edge of the trench, quite unconcerned at the German whiz-bangs that were coming over in salvos close to our heads. I can remember him saying, 'Yes, Sir, those were the happiest years of my life,' when describing his soldiering days in India. He asked permission of Colonel Griffin if he might put the pigeons inside the Headquarters dugout for protection. He thought they might get hurt if left out in the open trench.

Another unusual method used to send messages was by aeroplane, flying low and using a claxon horn to send out morse messages — very brief ones naturally. At other times, a message was dropped by a floater ribbon, a rather tedious and not very speedy way of relaying information and orders.

After our final attack near the chemical works, on 3 May, which was unsuccessful, we were sent back to rest in Arras. For our next line of duty we were sent south of the Scarpe, up on the hill in front of a village called Monchy Le Preux. Our orders were to hold the line in front of it. Being on high ground with plenty of dead land behind it, we could

walk about without being observed and it became quite a restful tour
of the trenches. We stayed in the Monchy area for the next two months,
backwards and forwards from our billets in Arras, then back into the line
either at Monchy or south of it. This country lay just north of Cambrai
where, in November, hundreds of tanks were deployed.

It was a quiet time about five miles behind the front and with very
little shelling. The trenches were summertime ones with rolling hills
between the river and the Somme — the lovely rolling hills, deep dugouts
and good trenches. It was all very different country from that around
Ypres where we all knew we would be involved sooner or later.

The third Ypres offensive, known popularly as the battle of
Passchendaele, commenced on 31 July in the most unfavourable
conditions of rain and mud; the drainage of the area had been destroyed
by shelling and had become a swamp. The Germans had machine-guns
in concrete pillboxes and mustard gas shelling was on a large scale, so
the British could only make limited advances with extremely heavy
bombardments — not the correct tactics over such unsuitable ground.
However, it wasn't until September that we received our marching orders,
trained, moved north and came behind the lines at Ypres. We went on
to the banks of the Zeer Canal as support for about a week, and then
we came out again prepared for the attack. The whole country in front
of Ypres was quite flat and was a mass of shell holes. There were none
of the deep dugouts that were part of the Somme country for the reason
that the chalk was not there; it was all mud and far too wet to dig.

We went up into the line on the night of 7/8 October. It was pitch
dark and it started to rain — as it always seemed to do when our turn
came. You might ask how, in that pitch-black wilderness, the formations
found their way. First of all, there were duckboard tracks laid literally
for miles and they were so slippery with the rain and mud that time and
again they became misplaced and a man would take a somersault sideways
onto his back. Many of the duckboards got buried in the holes or broke
up, with the result that units often lost their way. A scheme was therefore
devised by engineers whereby lines of tape were laid, stretching literally
for three to four miles, which the guides ran through their fingers. It was
a tough tape that couldn't be cut easily, and although initially white, was
soon mud coloured. Tapes were used in those areas which were used
at night and where the country was flat. The Germans had a regular
serried line of pillboxes about six feet high and of varying sizes depending
on whether they held machine-guns or as a shelter for a platoon of troops.
They were sombre places because they were half buried in mud. The
walls were anything up to five feet thick and it wasn't a very pleasant
experience sitting inside one of them. For one thing, the air was foul.

On the night we went up to the front, the troops took up their positions,
one company on the left flank and one on the right, with the other two
companies behind — one in support and one in reserve — all in an area
of, say, 500 yards.

The proposed advance, set to take place at dawn, had a fixed objective 1,500 yards ahead. The map was imprinted on my mind. About 2 a.m. I went to Batalion Headquarters where my friend Jim Watkins was in command. We were accompanied by his batman, my batman, the intelligence officer Chark, and a signal officer, Dave Gilmore. For the first hour the shelling was bad on the track, so we took shelter in one of the pillboxes which, of course, was occupied by our troops. Living in this for over an hour was an experience one would rather forget. It was supposed to hold from six to ten men and there were now about 30 in it. There was one candle in a bottle and this blew out when a shell landed on the roof or nearby and shook the whole structure. It was a great relief to leave it about 4 a.m. out into the fresh air again, and take up our position at the front, taking cover in a couple of big shell holes where we waited until the barrage began about 5.30 a.m.

Attacks had been recurring every few days up there. Whenever a big barrage started, the Germans knew an attack was imminent. With the ground so flat one had to creep forward just behind the barrage, and when it ceased, drop out of sight into a shell hole. For the first time in France we had on our left our sister battalion, the 1st Lancashire Fusiliers. They belonged to the famous 29th Division, which had made its name on Gallipoli. On their left was the Guards Division and further on the left were the French, attacking an area known as Houthulst forest.

It was barely daylight when the barrage began. It went on for about six minutes in front of us and then moved on and we continued behind it in the early morning light, advancing into the mist. I remember one fellow's water bottle being shot off his side but he just continued advancing. I tried to keep as close as I could to the colonel so that the men would know where to locate me, in the event of stretchers being needed.

We hadn't advanced very far when I found Watty's batman, a fellow by the name of Dunn, kneeling beside a German and in the dim light realised that both were dead. I could only surmise that Dunn had bent down to bandage the German who, being badly wounded, was bleeding profusely, when a shell struck nearby. Dunn was still holding the bandage in his hand. This kind act cost him his life.

As the light grew stronger I directed my eight stretcher-bearers to get into a big shell hole where we took shelter from the heavy machine-gun fire. There was a deep pool of water in the hole and so we arranged ourselves around the bank, and presently were shocked to see an aeroplane, with its painted black cross, flying low over us. We always took it for granted the low-flying aeroplanes were ours and were horrified to see that this was not. I shouted at the fellows to get down and keep still but the pilot had already spotted us. He circled round again and came right over us and dropped two bombs right on the edge of the crater. We were so very lucky we were only splattered with mud, and he didn't bother to come back again fortunately. As soon as we had the opportunity we climbed out of that shell hole and into another one.

I picked up various men whom I knew were wounded. Our stretcher-bearers did a wonderful job. Somehow we managed to get the wounded out of the front line while our troops advanced another 1,000 yards. Altogether it had not been a bad day. We had reached our objective and the fighting died down at nightfall.

I will never forget a friend of mine, Elkington, whom I found lying on the ground. He was a tall, thin fellow with a particularly grim face which now looked grimmer than ever. To my question if he were hurt, he replied, 'Only my arm. Lost it.' And, true enough, his arm had been blown off. We managed to patch him up, however, and home he went to England, and survived. At the time of my wedding, some years later, the men gave me a silver platter and Elkington's name is on it.

We were involved in two attacks with about a week's interval in between. My friend, Alan McDonald, came through both attacks safely, but Watty received a flesh wound in the upper arm during the second attack which was in much the same territory but without any significant advance. The Germans, again, had brought in reinforcements and strongly held their ground.

On 6 April 1917 U.S.A. declared war on Germany, but it was almost a year before any American troops set foot in Europe. After our second battle at Passchendaele in October, we pulled out with very depleted ranks and returned to our old haunts around Arras, to the country we had come to know so well and were even pleased to see again.

October and November 1917 were momentous months with success still favouring the Germans for the most part. First, there was the collapse of the Italian front, the Allied capture of Passchendaele and the ridge, the success of the opening phase of the Battle of Cambrai when so much of the German Hindenburg line was overrun. And last but not least the impending withdrawal of Russia from the war, after the Bolshevik revolution.

There used to be two sorts of raids, the silent raids and the noisy ones. Sometimes they were successful. The Army could never make up its mind which were the more successful — whether to take a chance at night without a bombardment, hoping to cut the wire first with wire cutters, or whether to have a bombardment which of course roused the enemy, and then to rush through. R.C. Sherriff's tragic play, *Journey's End*, had just such a raid for a subject and portrayed the sad fact that even they were hardly ever worth the loss of life they incurred.

The Brigade was still holding this sector when I left them on New Year's Day, 1918.

I was most upset at the way I was relieved of my duties. One night a medical officer arrived and told me that Divisional Headquarters had sent him to relieve me, and that I was to report back to Headquarters as soon as possible. We were holding the line right in front of Monchey and everything was fairly quiet. I promptly asked the signal officer to contact Divisional Headquarters to ascertain if it were true that I was to be relieved, and if so, I would prefer to go the following day after saying goodbye to everyone. Permission was granted for this delay.

I felt very strongly that I should have been informed of the proposed changeover. I had been with the Battalion for eighteen months and, as far as I was aware, no fault had been found with me. I was informed at Headquarters that my recall had been carried out with the best of intentions, the Director of Medical Services informed me later that he was convinced I was tired and in need of a well-earned rest. Be that as it may, I felt I should have been afforded the courtesy of being consulted about a transfer, and this had been denied me.

I went the rounds, saying goodbye to various people of differing ranks for whom I had affection and respect. I remember very distinctly saying farewell to John Carr, the Colonel's runner. He had been there with Captain Scott and Captain Tyrell before me. When I informed him I was going, he said, 'Oh, well, good luck to you'. I replied, 'I'm sorry I'm going. I'll be back one of these days, John.' His reply was 'No, you won'. When I enquired why he said that, he replied, 'Oh, they all says that. But none of them comes back.' I am happy to say that John saw the war through, along with his cobber, Dan Lonergan — one Lancashire and one Irish, but the best of pals.

We were unaware of it then, of course, but 1918 had dawned the beginning of the end.

Having said my adieus, I moved down the communication trench, all alone and feeling very lonely, for the three or four mile walk back to Arras and Divisional Headquarters. After spending the night in a billet in Arras I was taken by truck to Rouen and was then sent to a convalescent depot where there were three to four thousand troops recovering after release from hospital a few miles out of Rouen. The hospital was 40 miles behind the line, and after my front-line duties I found the somewhat bored, frivolous attitude of the officers and WAACS irritating in the extreme. I hated my time there and returned to England as soon as was possible.

As I mentioned earlier, when on leave the previous year in London I had attempted to join the AIF only to be told I would have to return to Australia and join up there. But on my return to London in 1918 I applied once again and this time was successful.

My first AIF posting was at Southall in London, to a rehabilitation hospital where a lot of Australian doctors were attending to amputation cases. After a fortnight there I was sent over to the first Australian General Hospital in Rouen.

I met some very fine Australian doctors in the AGH, including Alan Newton who was one of the surgical specialists. He was later knighted and became one of Melbourne's leading surgeons. In 1918 he was a captain and a most charming and interesting man to work with. He was most conscientious with his patients, and was at pains to help the younger men who were not so experienced in surgery. There was a lot of surgery to be performed in those days and, being rather a novice, I was given largely anaesthetics to do. I also looked after the wards, and during times of fierce fighting we were kept very busy with the large numbers of casualties.

Now, one or two things on the lighter side.

On one occasion we were honoured with a visit to the hospital by the Archbishop of Rouen. I happened to be on orderly duty at the time, along with a man by the name of Andy Brennan — a very cheerful Irish fellow, a very clever pathologist from Melbourne. The first we knew of His Grace's arrival was when the bugle blew and we had to return to the Orderly Room. We were informed of the Archbishop's visit and requested to do the honours. We set off along a path to greet a red-robed figure alighting from a motor car, and as we approached, he held out his hand to us. I cheerfully shook it, only to see Andy Brennan (being an RC) go down on one knee and kiss it!

I felt my position keenly. However, the Archbishop was an extremely pleasant gentleman — although we did have some difficulty with the language because he knew no English and we had only rusty French. I remember when I was showing him around my ward I presented the chart of a man with a high septic fever, and making conversation, murmured 'Coldstream Guards'. He replied, 'Oui, oui, oui,' running his fingers up and down the chart, and I don't know whether he thought I was saying 'Cold shivers' or what! Strange how one remembers these unimportant incidents.

Our life continued, sometimes quiet, sometimes hectic. If it were quiet we used to have a Saturday or Sunday off and would spend the day walking in the wonderful pine woods around Rouen, or went on some excursion down the River Seine to an old castle — Joumeaise, I think it was. It was the loveliest country in the summer — the antithesis of my life in the Flanders mud.

Our hospital, on the racecourse at Rouen, was situated amongst a cluster of hospitals. Right opposite was an American hospital, and the chief pathologist at the neighbouring British hospital was Charles Martin, later Sir Charles, who had been head of the Lister Institute in London and before that the Walter and Eliza Hall Institute in Melbourne. He was English, but always prided himself on being an Australian by adoption and would wear the Australian slouch hat. He was a large, rather plain man with a strong face like Jack Hawkins, and was very attached to this hat, not of course the proper dress for a British officer!

The war news was always with us, of course. With Russia's exit Germany had only to fight on one front and had transferred her Eastern divisions to France. We knew of the German assault on the British line on 21 March, aided by the early morning fogs, and its culmination two weeks later in a great defeat for the British. American divisions were arriving in increasing numbers, adding to Germany's urgency to serve a knockout blow to the British. In May the Marne was once again in the headlines, sending shivers down everyone's spines; however, the day was saved when the Allies counter-attacked successfully in July and August.

I found it desperately sad and depressing in the spring and summer when the Spanish flu struck — the most tragic thing I saw, battles and all. Men coming in from the battlefield, and those already in hospitals, died in inordinately high numbers from this pneumonic influenza, a severe viral infection of the lungs following flu. There were no antibiotics to counter secondary infections, though it was questionable how much the antibiotics would have helped, bearing in mind the infection was viral. Some of the poor fellows went stark, raving mad with it, with soaring temperatures; we had our work cut out trying to restrain them from getting out of bed, etc. The Army lost a tremendous number of men. Then, in autumn the flu struck the civilian populations worldwide — eventually tapering off in Sydney the following year.

On reflection, it was inevitable, I think, that due to the stress of that most horrid of wars, people's immune systems would break down under the strain.

We heard eventually that Paris was coming in for its share of bombardments, starting on Good Friday by Big Bertha, a huge German gun firing from approximately 70 miles away. Fortunately the air-raids over England had ceased in May.

If I'd realised how soon the war was going to be over I would have endeavoured to return to the front line where I felt I might have been of more use than as an assistant in this hospital. Also, my thoughts and feelings were so often with those I knew at the front; we seemed to be living such safe and comfortable lives at Rouen as there was no bombing in the back areas in those days.

We were particularly proud to learn of the elan of the Australian troops towards the end of August, and of their capture of Mt St Quentin in early September. We much admired the gallantry of the British 46th Division, also, in its assault on the Hindenburg system and were greatly cheered by the German retirement on the Argonne and later near Ypres.

The end, when it did come, came so abruptly. We heard about two days before the Armistice that the Germans were pulling back and then, all of a sudden, on 11 November it was all over and at 11 a.m. the church bells all over Rouen rang out, heralding peace. There was great jubilation that night where that morning there had been much solemnity. I remember one Tommy Atkins, however, who wasn't too solemn as he came running up the path waving a paper. 'It's all over, chum,' he said. 'It's all over!'

Although officially the war was over at 11 a.m. on 11 November 1918, the 'victorious' British and French Armies were almost broken and still had not penetrated German borders. Germany's Army, on the other hand, after the collapse of the Ottoman and Hapsburg Empires remained unbroken, everywhere on foreign soil. Quite recently I read Douglas Reed's book *Insanity Fair*, in which he claims Germany was never defeated. They cleverly bluffed their way into a peace, allowing the way open to renew hostilities 20 years later, with the surety of winning. Again, they almost did.

After the initial rejoicing, with crowds dancing in the streets, liquor flowing, the overall feeling settled down to one of immense relief that hostilities had ceased. I remember, however, that the American hospital had a dance one night and we all danced round to 'Over There' — 'The Yanks are Coming, The Yanks are Coming.' In moments of relief after stress, humans are apt to act in unbecoming ways, causing later regret, or at least embarrassment.

Our hospital was one of the first to be evacuated of wounded, the men being sent to Southampton by ship, via Rouen or Le Havre.

We remained a further two weeks and the time was spent in visiting the surrounding countryside and in agreeable pursuits. Rouen was a delightful city and, of course, still is. We took the opportunity of exploring some of its history, including its lovely cathedral, and we celebrated with concerts and quite disgraced ourselves with the stores, eating and drinking to our hearts' content, convinced we would not be able to take the remainder back to England with us. In this, of course, we were aided and abetted by our Mess Secretary, Dr Andrew Brennan.

Once back in England and settled into a miserably cold hospital hut at Warminster, a great sense of anti-climax set in. Our two-month stay on Salisbury Plain and Sutton Viney, with a hospital full of those suffering from the pneumonic epidemic, was not a very happy time. Apart from discomforts, there was the gnawing uncertainty of what we were to do next.

Some of the most vivid memories at this time concerned the German prisoners. One I particularly remember. He had been badly shot through the chest and it was touch and go whether he would survive. We had no penicillin or antibiotics, of course, and he had to battle for his life, but all the time he was so very polite and grateful for all that was done for him.

The returning troops were full of stories of incidents in the front line. One sergeant told me of an occasion when a dugout had become filled in after a shell exploded. A lot of men had been buried, so he had arranged for reinforcements to uncover them. They eventually made a small hole so they could speak to the imprisoned men. In answer to the sergeant's, 'Who's in charge there?' an Australian voice responded, 'I am, Corporal —.' The sergeant continued, 'Well, have you got any married men there?' The reply came back. 'Yes, there is one fellow here. Joe somebody.' 'Well, send him up. Married men first.' Fortunately the incident ended happily with all men rescued.

The general restlessness I referred to at Sutton Viney was a natural reaction to war's end. The first four years of my career had been concentrated in a war that was never going to end. When it did, one was left floundering, wondering in which direction one should go. This uncertainty was aggravated by the fact that, in a sense, one was stranded in Britain. There were thousands of troops from the Empire countries to be repatriated but, due to the submarine war, there were not nearly enough ships to take them home.

When it was realised that it would be months before the many thousands of troops could embark, the Army, for once, hit upon a really sensible plan of educational leave to officers and men. If you could present a good case that you were studying some peacetime course, or wished to study one, you were given six months off to pursue the course on normal army pay. After six months, it was hoped that you could be shipped home.

Again, Jack Morlet persuaded me to join him, this time at the Royal Northern Hospital. Just as we schemed to be together at Eastbourne in 1915, so now we schemed together to get me into the Royal Northern, where we spent the next six months. Of the surgeons at this hospital, I remember there was a Mr Sherran, who wrote a textbook on surgery, and a very fine and friendly New Zealander, a Mr Choice, who wrote a book called *Choice's Surgery*. Also in London at that time was Thomas Dunhill, a well-known Australian surgeon who had made his name performing thyroid gland operations.

The six months were the usual busy hospital routine, with weekends off. Our pay was one pound a week, which was in addition to our Army pay.

During this time, the unthinkable happened: British labour went on strike in London. I remember there was a meeting at the Royal Northern to consider whether or not doctors should retaliate by refusing to treat strikers or their families. Mr Choice summed up the situation most succinctly when he said that he did not care one way or the other whether a man was a striker or not: if he came into the hospital with a strangulated hernia, he would operate. As medicos, we felt we had no alternative.

Eventually, my six months hospital duty ended and my sister Ena and I went on a tour of the English Lakes District. We also met and stayed at the McKies at Bishopton on the Clyde below Glasgow. The reason for our visit here was that my other sister, in Australia, had become engaged to Tom McKie, a Scotsman who had gone to Australia as a railway engineer in 1910, and like most Britons in Australia, had joined up with the AIF.

Tom McKie was invalided through a wound and had gone back to Australia. My mother was a member of the Red Cross and arranged for him to stay at a cottage she had at Leura — she often used to take soldiers who had no home for a week's holiday in the mountains. They became very fond of Tom. He came back several times and eventually became engaged to my elder sister Zelda.

The general atmosphere in London in the months before our return was very much one of business as usual. I think this was a great failing and that few people realised that Britain had raised the largest volunteer army the world had ever seen. I don't think volunteers will come forward in the same numbers again — nearly 1,000,000 men. The steadfastness of those men, their magnificent loyalty and sense of duty and sheer endurance, was something that passes understanding. There was something very special about the British Tommy — an extraordinary stubbornness and patience — and I think there were comparatively few people who really were aware of all that the war entailed. True, there were rationing and bombings, but it was really those who had men at the front who bore the real brunt of the war.

Being Australian in those days meant also that we were very proud of our British roots. We used to believe that Britons were the salt of the earth. I appreciate that, nowadays, this sounds boastful and egotistical but we were then proud of our country and proud of being British. They felt Britain had something to offer the world in the way of personal freedom and justice, law and order, and I think this had a lot to do with the way men flocked to the colours.

In Australia there was a far greater appreciation of men who had volunteered than there was in Britain. They had not considered their own careers but had gone off, perhaps with various motives; but behind them all was the feeling that it was the right thing to do and having got there, all displayed a most remarkable spirit of 'sticking it out'. It was rare to find anyone who tried to evade his responsibilities — while his mates were there he felt he couldn't leave.

Social affairs were very much more incorporated in Australian law than in British law. Returned soldiers were generously treated in this country by the government but not so in Britain, except by private organisations. British soldiers appeared to accept this attitude. After all, Britain had taken so many knocks throughout history, and the soldier took it all as part of life; one war was the same as another, and they didn't appear to expect any returns or any compensation for what they had been through. It is my view, however, that parliament and the people generally should have seen to it that their fighting men were adequately compensated.

Never were so many lives lost by so much bungling for so little gain.

Thus ended Armageddon, or the war to end all wars. And yet within two decades the whole tragic saga was to be repeated: in the west by Germany, continuing where she had left off twenty years earlier; and in the east by Japan, rampaging through China and igniting the whole Pacific region ... and with a toehold at our back door.

Captain Huxtable on his favourite horse, Sailor, in 1915

A very tired medical officer

Charles Huxtable with his children, just before leaving for Singapore

PART TWO

Malaya and Singapore, 1941-42

After the Fall of Singapore Dr Huxtable wrote an account of his time on the Island and of general lack of preparedness for the imminent Japanese invasion, which he concluded with a stinging attack on what he saw as a cynicism and degeneracy in the democracies. In both this account, and the diary entries that follow, it will be seen that he returned to these pages, adding notes and perspectives that round out his opinions but that seem at first to be out of chronological sequence.

After twenty years of general practice in medicine I went to Melbourne and enlisted in the Second AIF with the rank of Captain. I sailed in the hospital ship *Wanganella* from Sydney on Saturday, 30 August 1941. After calling at Melbourne and Perth, we set out for Malaya with all lights blazing, portholes open, Red Cross flag flying, and no convoy. Nobody was troubled by any possibility of violation of the Geneva Convention.

We arrived at Singapore on 14 September, after passing the mountainous coast of Java where we saw spray on the cliffs, a lighthouse in the Banda Straits and flat Sumatra beyond, but had no view of Krakatoa, the volcano. We continued through the shimmering haze and the flat landscapes bounding the Banka Strait, the shallow waters of which lie between Banka Island and Sumatra. Green islands were dotted everywhere, as were Malay praus, Chinese junks and sampans.

We crossed the narrow channel to Singapore's harbour with its colourful shores and soon tied up at the wharf. There were general goodbyes and goodluck wishes and then it was down the gangway to set foot in Malaya. Among the first of the staff on board was our old friend, 'Billy' Kent Hughes,* DAOMG and, so by motor buses along seven miles of bitumen through the historic city, we eventually reached our billets in the fine three-storeyed buildings comprising St Patrick's School on the East Coast Road.

We settled in comfortably, with plenty of room to spare. In front, on

*Wilfrid Selwyn Kent Hughes, Rhodes Scholar, Olympic athlete and later MHR and Federal minister. In 1946 he published *Slaves of the Samurai*, an epic poem written surreptitiously while a POW.

the south side, was the sea. It was only a few yards away, but cut off from us by barbed wire, land mines and numerous notices which read 'Danger. Keep Away.' On the opposite side, between piles of buildings and the main east coast road, were 150 yards of fine 'padang' or playing fields, fringed by trees. To the east were strong points for defence: a broad, deep drain — evil-smelling at times and also fringed by barbed wire — and slit trenches for air raids. Beyond the drain were a coconut grove and tumble-down native sheds and huts. To the west, that is, in the direction of Singapore City, a row of pleasant villas faced the barbed wire and the beach.

The men slept on the two upper storeys of the north building. Parallel to that was the south building near the beach, occupied by the nursing staff. Matron Drummond joined us after our arrival and took command of the latter, while our CO, Colonel Pigdon, arrived about the same time from the Australian Convalescent Depot further up the west coast (Batu Pahat), having given up the command there to take charge of our newly arrived unit. A Melbourne man, he was a returned soldier (gunner) of the last war.

The Officers' Mess was a pleasant spot on the ground floor under the sisters' quarters, with wide doors looking out over the bay to the groups of islands seven or eight miles away, and the numerous native fish-trap dwellings erected on crazy sticks standing in the shallow water. The two parallel main buildings are joined at their centre by a wing built at right angles to each and comprise a large chapel above and a very spacious lounge below which we had very comfortably furnished by the Army authorities. It was too large for the officers, however, and later the colonel had one end changed to a concert hall for the men. Here we had several entertainments from visiting troops and civilians from Singapore.

The first nights seemed fairly hot, tropical and airless, but not as oppressive as one had been led to believe. The climate in this country had been exaggerated and condemned in advance, or so it seemed to me as time went on. Personally, I never catch a cold here. There is an absence of wind and of dust, and few flies or other pests except where the Army breeds them. The most common small animal is the friendly, light-coloured ubiquitous little chee cha, a small variety of lizard which chirps cheerily from the walls and whose consummate skill in running upside down across the ceilings and rushing headfirst down vertical walls continually amazes us.

One person I had learnt to know in bygone army days was the habitual moaner — one who always expects his food and his personal comfort to be 'just so', but who never offers his help in arranging a menu to suit everybody, and who would never think of saying 'thank you' to the cook on those occasions when a meal has been particularly good. Fortunately, there were only one or two of those and, for the most part, we were a happy crowd of holiday-makers during those first three months in Singapore. For the balloon did not go up on 15 September; we had to wait until 8 December for that, and many of us hoped it would not come. However, this was wishful thinking, and I believe now that the inevitability of war should have been obvious to everyone.

Little did we think at this time that the General Hospital, only four months later, would be thrown out of Johore and crowded back, with its 400 to 500 wounded, into these very same buildings before the victorious advance of the Japanese Army. Little could we know that we would witness here, in these peaceful surroundings, the final tragic fortnight before the surrender and the week following when, as prisoners of war pondering our fate, we finally departed — a disheartened and almost disorganised cavalcade of sick, wounded medical personnel (minus nurses) — for our final prisoner-of-war quarters at Changi.

During these peaceful days from September to November, there were such unimportant things to discuss and argue as the correct manner of salute parades and formations on the padang, the correct stick drill for officers, the correct way to hold a swagger cane when standing at ease — should it be under the armpit or behind the back! There were sightseeing tours of Singapore city and round the island which is approximately 25 miles east to west and 15 miles north to south. There were entertainments at tennis at lovely private houses on the outskirts of the city such as at Dr John's house and at the home of Mr Howl, the Attorney-General, whose lovely green grass courts spread out beneath the picturesque albrizzia trees, where bougainvillea, *Bignonia venusta*, hibiscus, orchids and frangipani added their fragrance. There were dinners, swims and one or two dances at the fairyland known as the Swimming Club, at the Airport Hotel and other places where the menus were as long as a small magazine.

The nurses, needless to say, were entertained like princesses, partly owing to their own charms and partly to the fact that unmarried ladies were at a premium in this place where, all told, the European population of the Island was only 9,000 as against 400,000 Chinese and 90,000 Malays.

I visited the interesting Raffles Museum, with the particularly fine Raffles Library upstairs and I read, with many thrills, the amazing career of that great Englishman who founded Singapore 120-odd years ago.

Also during these weeks we had interesting clinics at different hospitals in the city. I went two or three times to the Alexandra Military Hospital (where later there was a tragedy involving several medical officers just prior to the surrender). Here, Major Colder, the pathologist, showed us malarial films. Then, on Friday afternoons, Major Bruce Hunt (ever in the lead with all flags flying) would lead a party of us to a clinic at the Tan Tock Sang Hospital where the leaders were Professor Ransom and Dr Wallace, in association with Major Hunt.

I spent an interesting afternoon with some of the others at the Singapore General Hospital, where we saw a good many beri-beri and typhoid patients (mostly Chinese). Afterwards, there followed a very pleasant afternoon tea party with our demonstrator, Dr Landor, at his residence in the Hospital grounds. His wife and family, as was the case of so many men here, had gone to Australia. On this occasion, I was honoured by the presence of the Matron and the Assistant Matron. The Matron, though not slim, dances very well and very lightly, and, what surprised me more, ordered a pot of beer at dinner. We saw Billy Kent Hughes swinging around to the absurdly fast waltz time which the orchestras beat out in this part of the world.

The Swimming Club made us honorary members, so although we paid highly for entertainment there, we do not pay quite as much as the civilian population.

During these halcyon days and nights, one never really felt the heat, partly owing, I suppose, to little work and nearly all holiday.

We had several meetings with Lieutenant and Mrs Wilkinson and some young Australian Officers from the RAN corvette *Burnie*. The corvette, *Goulburn* was also in the vicinity. Later, I heard that *Burnie* reached Darwin after the capitulation, but did not hear the fate of *Goulburn*.

One night the Wilkinsons took me to dinner with a middle-aged Scot, Mr Baillie, a widower or grass widower if not a bachelor, in a fine house somewhere in the Holland Road district where there are many fine houses with sweeping lawns, park-like gardens, spreading albrizzia trees, shrubs and frangipani. Finally, about 10 p.m. Mr Baillie asked Mrs Wilkinson if she thought it was too early to commence dinner. To my relief, she said 'no' — that, in fact, she was feeling 'peckish'. We then passed through an arcade to an adjoining room where the silent-footed waiter cum cook again appeared but, to my dismay, with no food. Mr Baillie then asked us in turn what we would like to eat; anything we fancied, in fact. In desperation, and with calculation, I plumped for bacon and eggs. Mr Baillie thought this a very good suggestion provided I had sausages as well. This appealed to me enormously and in a few minutes I was delighted to see my order appear through the doorway.

As may be gathered, life in Singapore continued as usual, regardless of the gathering storm clouds. To be honest, I think that most of us in the Army, no less than the civilian population, clung to the belief that the Japanese were only bluffing and would not strike; the northern borders were 600-700 miles away; the Siamese were pro-British; Singapore was a fortress; and that the defence of Johore was safe in the hands of the Australian 8th Division (2 Brigades)!

I did hear it said on occasions that the defence of the east coast of Johore by one brigade only was rather a tall order, and when I visited Mersing in October (a day trip) and later in November for three weeks, I was made very much aware of the inadequacy of our defence; uncomfortably so. I had this same painful awareness on my first arrival on Singapore Island, when I found that the total garrison of the 'fortress' was only 3,000 troops — just three British battalions; the 1st Gordons, the 2nd Argyles and the 1st Manchesters. The gallant North Lancashire

Regiment had been there as well, it is true, but they were moved up the peninsula early. Nevertheless, one was lulled by the air of laissez-faire in the community, of confidence in some hidden defence measures which we had up our sleeve, so to speak, by a false confidence that the prestige of the U.S.A. alone would restrain the Japanese and that Siam offered a barrier to Japan.

The AIF rank and file were all confident that if the Japanese *did* come, well it would be too bad for *them!* One young AIF officer, who had been attached to British units up on the Siamese border, assured me that we (that is, the British Army) had several divisions up there and thousands of Indians. I plead this false idea of the British strength up north as a partial excuse for my own share in the widespread stupidity and lack of judgement that led to the downfall of Malaya.

Perhaps it is pertinent to insert here the salient facts about the shocking collapse of Malayan defence, this rapid disintegration of the British Empire in the Far East and the loss of the Dutch East Indies, with its accompanying blow to the prestige of both the British Commonwealth of Nations and the United States. From the Australian point of view, it also meant the exposure of our homeland to possible attack by Japanese forces.

Over the years there has been a degeneracy in the democracies, an undue emphasis on the horrors of war and peace at any price; a cynicism about the need for, or even the existence of, any international or political morality; the stepping aside from the pathway of the bully and, in some quarters, the parading of such humiliation as a Christian virtue. Have our churches, for instance, forgotten, or have they never realised, that the appeal of Christianity is to heroism? If the manner of Christ's death does not teach men how to die for truth and for principle, then what need was there for him to die a violent death?

The religion of many inside the churches, no less than the cynicism of those outside them, appears to be based upon a conception of the crucifixion that reduces its idealism to a mere exhibition of sensationalism and emotionalism. Where are the Rupert Brookes of this war? Where are the Julian Grenfells? Modern youth, broadly speaking, has been taught to belittle military virtue, to deprecate, if not to despise, heroics. Can he be altogether blamed if he has taken his lead from elders who have turned their backs on the sacrifices made in their generation and who:

> in the Churches, have preached a Christianity which is false in that it is timid;

> in public life and parliament, have dealt lightly with dishonesty, corruption and bribery;

> in schools have often paid tribute to a form of Communism which is not Christian and altruistic, but avowedly materialistic and Godless;

> in the professional and businesslike world, have held that career and capital are the two great pointers to a man's heaven.

How the great Schiller must have lamented in spirit when the land of Czechoslovakia was sacrificed by all the so-called democracies of the world (not by England and France alone, as taught by some Communists and others) into the blood-stained hands of Hitler. It was Schiller who wrote: 'Der tapfere Mann denkt an sich selbst zuletzt: vertraut auf Gott und rettet den Bedrängten'. (The brave man thinks last of himself: trusts in God and goes to rescue him who is oppressed.) Thus spoke his hero, Wilhelm Tell, and thus did President Benes appeal, in vain, to the other nations.

Although the general public in the democracies were woefully ignorant of their own countries' military weaknesses and the dictator countries' military strength, public opinion in those democracies showed a willingness to compromise with evil rather than stand up to it, to shake hands with the bully rather than oppose him. This lack of moral fibre and principle revealed itself in a number of ways, one example being the number of medical officers volunteering for service overseas.

In May 1940, during three black weeks of the Empire's history, 230 medical personnel, out of 6,000 in Australia, volunteered to serve abroad. of this 230, 17 were under 30 years of age. This contrasts sharply with the first eight months of the first war when not only were large numbers of young medical officers in Australia volunteering to help overseas with the AIF, but also 100 young medical men, early in 1915, volunteered to serve with the Royal Army Medical Corps.

There can be no doubt that leftists and their libraries and clubs and their so-called Communism have had a certain baneful influence on this lowered morale in our own country as also in France, England, America and elsewhere. Many well-meaning but immature minds were deceived into a kind of disloyalty to their country and kinsmen by the high-sounding praises and professed altruism of political agitators who styled themselves socialists, near-Communists or whole-hearted Reds.

So much for the decline of democracy. As it relates to the present humiliation in the Far East, suffice it to say that, in Malaya, there was not only a lack of adequate preparation for defence, but also weakness and irresolution in the local command (civil and military) and apathy amongst the civil population in the cities.

In Australia we continued to look inward and downward, rather than outward and upward at the war clouds gathering since 1937. What Australian government, for instance, would have dared propose, during the era of crisis prior to September 1939, that Australia had a direct responsibility, in men and money, for the defence of Singapore!

In the United States, the isolationists strove to deflect the majority public opinion away from foreign responsibilities, whilst the far-sighted Americans were only content to counter, by boast and threat, the continued infiltration of large numbers of Japanese into Indo China during the whole of the latter half of 1941. Had American armies and planes been sent to Malaya, Burma and the Dutch East Indies, when requested by these countries, the present debacle, in all probability, would never have occurred.

One salient fact of our predicament has been the lack of air defence in Malaya. I have seen in Johore, during the last weeks, frantic efforts made to complete airfields that should have been completed a year ago. I have heard from higher authority just how unaware we were of Japanese preparations in Thailand. I have spoken to dozens of our soldiers from the front — both AIF soldiers and British Tommies who had fought a rearguard action from 8 December on the Thai border down to the entrance of the enemy into Johore in mid-January, when they were relieved by the AIF, and in every instance there has been the one complaint:

'We never knew where the Japanese were. We only saw a plane of ours once or twice, whereas, all day long, the Japanese planes flew over us, skimming the tree-tops, locating us wherever we hid, bombing us, machine-gunning us, directing their artillery and mortars on us, driving our transport and supplies from the roads.'

There were not enough airfields, and those that did exist on the peninsula were so placed that they fell as easy prize to the enemy — for example, those at Sahro and Kuantan on the lonely and undefended east coast. There were not enough troops or ground defence to guard what airfields there were, and there were too few planes. Grand and heroic stands were made, such as the Argyles at Telokanson and the AIF on the Muar Road in front of Yong Peng and Parit Sulong where the 29th and 19th Battalions suffered a week of fiery ordeal by battle seldom equalled during the last war.

Field and machine-guns were generally without targets because, in that densely covered country, there were no aeroplanes to be the army's eyes. Confusion prevailed, too, in the higher commands, with confused, indefinite or irresolute orders. This 'blindfold' fighting, not knowing what was happening elsewhere, was too much for Indian troops. Small detachments of Japanese, with incredible skill and speed, outflanked them, and using fireworks and crackers to supplement their yells and rifle fire, often succeeded in giving the impression of complete encirclement. At night this led to wild and indiscriminate firing by the Indians and sometimes an outbreak of jitteriness and stampeding.

Another salient factor was the complete lack of static defence for Singapore Island from the north. The High Command had laid their 'Maginot Line' of barbed wire and land mines along the sea beaches on the south and east, but Johore, its vital naval base, was completely undefended from the north. Those responsible failed to visualise an enemy advance down the peninsula from the north or, if such a danger were known, no defence plans were made for such a contingency.

In that last fatal week of fighting, our men had to guard 20 to 30 miles of coastline that was obscured by mangroves and indented by creeks, without wire or prepared defences of any kind, whilst facing an enemy position that was, in many places, only separated from them by a few hundred yards of shallow water. To give an example of just one such hopeless situation — one Australian brigade, the 22nd Brigade, was given a front of 16,000 yards to defend, an impossible task.

Little did any of us know, at the end of that fateful week, that we were to remain as 'guests' of the Japanese for the ensuing three years.

1942

The Battle of Singapore Island and the Capitulation

31 January — 1 February
Looking across the water to the south, early this morning, one could see through the haze, this side of the Island, the grotesque shape of a mighty floating crane. This paradoxically buoyant object was apparently reaching its journey's end after a night voyage round from the naval base in the tow of a comparatively small tug, thus depriving the Japanese of a war prize of no mean dimension. Two hours later it was almost out of sight near a small island to the west and by that time a large three-funnel steamer was disappearing to the south-east bound for who knows where, perhaps Australia, India, or even America but, wherever bound, bravely facing the present-day perils of air, ocean and submarine.

As regards our hospital, there is a lull in the arrival of our wounded. The dangerously ill in our ward still fight their battle for life silently and uncomplainingly, some with grievous abdominal wounds.

Chief in our thoughts of such battlers is the young artillery officer of the 2/15th Regiment, Rabett, son of Rex Rabett of Sydney and nephew of a fellow collegiate of St Paul's College of 32 years ago. This uncle, when in college, we were wont to chaff because of his touch of the Beau Brummel and dandy, but in 1915 he proved his manhood as an officer in the Royal Artillery — a service to which another collegiate and contemporary, Adrian Consett Stephen,* devoted and gave his life. And so this fine young man, Rabett, is likely to give his, for his handsome face with its firm jaw and small trim moustache is becoming daily more

---

*Adrian Consett Stephen, MC, Croix de Guerre, a young Sydney solicitor who had shown considerable literary potential, was killed in action in March 1917. Dr Huxtable married his cousin, Barbara Rowan.

hollow and drawn by the struggle. Mercifully he retains hope and optimism and chaffs the surgeons in a weak voice calling them plumbers and telling me that his Uncle Bob is again in England serving in some capacity and had sent a cable to him in Malaya.

Another battler is a large-framed boy with blue eyes and fine teeth, Private Moffitt, also of the 2/15th Artillery.

Again, there is Sergeant Butt of Artarmon, with a bad chest wound, sitting bolt upright in bed, blue-tinged in spite of oxygen, breathless and unfailingly polite and courteous to sisters, orderly or doctor in every little request and acknowledgement. One prays that he, too, will get better.

There is nothing more touching than to receive gratitude from a wounded soldier when one is conscious of how very much is owed to them by us.

Without papers, without wireless, there are rumours in the air. The Japanese are in Johore Bahru, the troops have withdrawn, the causeway, which we left only last Monday, has been blown up. At 10 p.m., before turning into bed, I stood long under the brilliant moon filtering through the palm grove separating the main hospital buildings from the moonlit gardens of this really delightful Chinese residence which we are using as an Officers' Mess and billet. A soft carpet of couch grass underfoot, a cloudless moonlit sky above, in front silvery waters lapping softly on the beach extend eastwards towards Changi and westwards towards the city; but my thoughts and prayers turn south-east towards home. A few yards in front of me grim reminders of reality are the ugly concertina coils of barbed wire and the little dotted mole heaps where the land mines are laid. But, in spite of such a foregound, something of the peace which passeth all understanding descends from eternity above and beyond.

Two hours later there were ear-splitting crashes — four or more in quick succession coming closer, the last seemingly on top of this house, malicious and deafening in its impact and followed by sounds of falling debris. Everybody is tumbling out of the huts. Pyjamas and boots, shouts and running in the bright moonlight. It is our first contact with the enemy. The drone of the raider has died away and the experience has come and gone in a few minutes, but it has ushered in 1 February, and the seige of Singapore.

I join the stream of half-clad men who are making towards the south-east corner of the hospital building and there the stream emerges into a bewildered group looking up at a shattered top corner of the front of the building where the skeleton of a portion of the roof is silhouetted against the sky and whence sounds of water come splashing down. I find myself beside young Drevermann of Melbourne. 'Looks like your ward, Charles,' he says.

Running up two flights of stone steps I find my patients out of bed — 50 to 100 men rudely awakened from sleep and ruefully contemplating the hole in the corner of the roof through which poured torrents of water rapidly flooding the floor.

A few sturdy jokes and casual comments from among the men themselves soon causes the excitement to abate whilst two or three bleeding from scratches are taken below to be dressed. Sister Forsyth, just come from Australia, is calm and collected and is comforting a man who is unnerved, having lost an eye from a bomb wound at the front. Not much can be done before morning, beyond turning off the water supply at the main and going to bed again, this time to think, and then push aside the thought with a shudder: what if that bomb had struck the middle of the ward?

Later, at breakfast, we read in the papers that the causeway to Johore had indeed been blown up in the early hours, after all our troops had been withdrawn. The honour of defending the bridgehead to the last was given to the Argyle and Sutherland Highlanders. The siege of Singapore has really begun with the first day of February. There is an inspiring message from the Governor, Sir Shenton Thomas. We read the strange and, to me, interesting news that General Gordon Bennett called to say goodbye, perhaps 'au revoir', to the Sultan of Johore and to thank him for his generosity to the AIF. The Sultan certainly was generous to the hospital, presenting us with several valuable items including two X-ray outfits which we have with us here.

Today there is a cleaning up of the ward floor from the bomb debris, the removal of loose tiles and covering the gap with tarpaulin. I saw Tony Rabett and, after assuring me he was comfortable, I asked him if he would like me to write to his father; he declined, however, saying it might only worry them.

This morning (still the 1st), we saw, from our porch, a fine big three-funnel steamer putting out to sea. What ship is that? Some say the *Mary*. I wonder. Later, I had a telephone message — 'A friend of yours wants to speak to you on the telephone'. A voice from Southport and home, Alex Reed. He and Jock White are at General Base Depot on this island, having arrived with reinforcements — poor fellows, why didn't they return with their ship? Never mind, here they are, and I must go to see them; for Jack has only recently seen Barbara and the children at Mount Tamborine.

A quiet night followed the day, but there was no sleep for me before midnight, as I am Admitting Officer and 20 or more casualties arrived late, men with fevers, approximately 50 percent having malaria. The harvest of the anopheles now begins, after the weeks of sleeping, marching and fighting in swamps and jungles. One can only hope that the Japanese are succumbing in greater numbers than we are.

2 February
Today has dawned fine and clear. A large column of black smoke has been rising from the due north since yesterday and sweeping away to form a dense pall over the city to the west. Our residence has a semi-circular tiled porch with steps leading to a circular walk among the lawns

in front. The walk is flanked by curved stone seats beloved in Chinese architecture but is now out of bounds owing to the barbed-wire fence and minefield; however, it is pleasant to the eye nonetheless.

Looking across this foreground over the islands' dotted waters, we can often see the movement of ships coming and going, chiefly going. About 1.30 p.m., after lunch, another large three-funnelled passenger ship was hauled down to the south-east, whilst a few miles in her wake, just opposite us, was a large tanker heading full speed for the open seas. Meanwhile, the drone of a large formation of enemy bombers could be heard in the clouds above and one prayed for those gallant ships and the prayer was answered for the bombers, savagely intent on their target in the city, took no account of the ships. Following their usual custom, the whole load of bombs was released at once.

Captain Tony Rabbett died at 2.30 p.m. today; also the fine young gunner, Moffitt. Sergeant Butt still fights on — Colonel Charles Osborn operated today to remove a piece of shell fragment, three inches long, from behind the left side of his chest.

3 February

Two more ships passed out to sea today, one a high troop passenger, probably Dutch, good luck to them. The columns of smoke still rise from the same part of the city and also from the north, the latter due to our destruction of oil stores at the former naval base — now, alas, a thing of the past.

We have acquired a small yellow pup, thin and mangy, for a mascot. The domestic fly seems to be increasing in numbers and there are also a few green blowflies about. As I have remarked before, in letters home, Malaya is singularly free from pests when compared to Queensland. The absence of horses may have something to do with freedom from flies. Mosquitoes are seldom annoying in spite of the wet climate. Effective drainage, coupled with occasional deluges of rain, perhaps kills the larvae.

It is strange being back at St Patrick's School, the same quarters which we occupied on our arrival in Malaya. The place is now fitted up as a hospital, crowded with patients, and the large room in the basement, which served formerly as our First Officers' Mess of this unit, is now fitted up as an operating theatre with four tables. The Tenth AGH, our sister hospital in Malaya, is situated some miles away on this island. Our brief association with a dozen of their officers outside Johore Bahru was very pleasant in spite of daily worsening war news during that period. These officers came to us when the 10th had to clear out of Malacca before the advancing Japanese early in January, and included Carl Furner of Newcastle, Cotter Harvey of Sydney, Adrian Farmer of Melbourne, Claffey — eye specialist of Sydney, Captain Puflett of Sydney, Colonel Coates of Melbourne, Major Eagan of Sydney.

Strange to reflect that our atap mess hut, which was located up there early on 26 January, is now probably used by Japanese troops and all those large empty wards, handed over to us by the Johore new Mental Hospital and recently filled with Australian sick and wounded, were occupied five days later by Japanese troops. What is the fate of the civilian population of Johore Bahru and of that beautiful modern hospital of 1,000 beds?

4 February

Last night, a full brilliant moon arose in a cloudless sky — I never thought before that I could positively dislike the moon. Nevertheless, Tojo left us alone and the night was peaceful except that, in the early hours, the distant boom made the islands tremble and woke me for a few minutes. This morning there was no comment about it. In the morning's paper we read that airmail with Australia is temporarily suspended. That is rather depressing news. It follows the loss of a Qantas flying boat at Timor and all 13 lives on board. About 9 a.m. a formation flight of nine enemy bombers came over from west to east and we took to the trenches for a few minutes to avoid splinters from anti-aircraft fire.

From Ward H at the top of the building there is a grand view of sea and island and the distant city and harbour. With my field glasses I can see nine small ships and five fairly large ones at anchor and, against some blackened and ruined walls or go-downs, the skeletons of two burned-out ships.

My wards were finished by lunchtime and this afternoon I had two small peacetime operations. We have had plenty of admissions as regards medical cases but no wounded for several days. During the afternoon, Captain Cahill, Medical Officer of the now famous 2/19th Battalion, introduced me to Colonel Anderson, the CO. Anderson is a sturdy man with myopic glasses, a strong face, square chin with a dimple, pleasant manner and a rather English voice. He is a grazier from New South Wales.

Sitting amongst the garden shrubs and the *Bignonia venusta* where it adorns, and even in parts hides, the barbed wire under its lovely mantle of pink and green, there is lively bird life. Some are little crested honeyeaters the size of a sparrow, brown-backed and light-breasted. Some are larger brown-backed birds with white ears and a black horizontal bar below the ears. Still others I discovered, with something of a thrill, are our Queensland rainbow birds — the brilliant green backs and spiky tails aroused my suspicions which were soon confirmed with my field glasses.

5 February

In the early hours the siren wailed over Singapore and, hearing planes somewhere in the sky, we all turned out in pyjamas and tin hats and made for the trenches situated between outhuts and the main hospital building. Soon the rockets howling and the unnecessarily prolonged 'all-clear' wailed us all into bed again. The morning papers told us that the effects of the enemy fire are negligible up to date, but I am expecting some day that the outbreak of that continuous bombardment will herald the real Japanese assaults. It would be more comforting if the Straits of Johore was more than 1,100 yards in width at the causeway.

However, there are several bright spots. First, we know that a couple of days before we left Tampoi Johore Bahru, that is, about January 23, an Australian machine-gun battalion arrived from overseas. We have some officers with us who travelled with it, namely Major Watson, ear, nose and throat specialist from Sydney, Major Eddy of Sydney and Mr Wilson of the Red Cross. I have since heard by telephone from General Base Depot, now situated on the island, from Alex Reed of Southport. He and Jock White of Tamborine were also in the same convoy. Second, a week ago today there was a convoy in the harbour and Padre Usher, who was in town, saw truckloads of British and Indian troops just arriving. Third, there are some Hurricanes in the sky these days. Not enough certainly, but still some.

Over and above these hopeful signs there is the battle of Bataan. General MacArthur is surely one of the most heroic military figures in history and we all admire him and those in his command. Had they not fought as they have, Japanese landing barges with invasion forces would have been loosed against us. Not only has he held them at bay, but he destroyed such large numbers that his stand denied the Japanese warships the use of Manila Bay.

One night in November, in Mersing, I saw at an army cinema Dumas' *Man in the Iron Mask*. Caught in a desperate situation, D'Artagnan says to the elderly Cardinal, 'That, with courage, they will face what comes'. 'Ah, my friend,' says the Cardinal, 'bravery is a great thing when there is hope'. D'Artagnan replied, 'bravery is only a great thing when there is no hope'. Such is the high idealism which inspired General MacArthur when he said, 'only those willing to die are fit to live'. Such men are the salt of a nation and the only hope in times like these. In every democratic country a cancer seems to have bitten deep. It seemed to grow 24 years ago when the dead began to be forgotten except by those who had lost them, and cynicism defiled the cause for which they had died. It seems that self-advancement has become the religion of the serious-minded and self-indulgence the religion of youth. Alfred Noyes expressed it thus:

The cymbals clash and dancers walk
With long silk stockings and arms of chalk.
Butterfly skirts and white breasts bare
And shadows of dead men watching them there.

Mr Curtin and Mr Forde have sent inspiring messages to approximately 15,000 Australians on the front line, calling them patriots, and yet only a few years before war broke out no Labour leader in Australia would have dared to urge men to fight abroad for the British Empire. It is to be hoped that such narrow isolationism has left our country forever and that we shall be prepared to shoulder our responsibilities henceforth towards the great association of democratic nations which is the British Empire.

This morning at 11 a.m. 'Tojo' paid us his usual morning visit. A formation of nine bombers flew over from east to west, dropping a salvo of bombs on the airport two miles down the road. The other day I operated for osteomyelitis in the femur of young Sergeant Griffin.* A few days later he asked me whether I was any relation to Ena Huxtable and, since then, we have had many cheery talks about Leura and the days after the last war when he lived there and knew the Mort family and all our other friends.

Things have been cheered and brightened 100 percent, in the last couple of days, by a long letter from Barbara from Eagle Heights and from mother from Toowoomba. Mater tells me that Tom McKie has been entraining American soldiers which is very good and interesting news. We knew that sailors had arrived.

6 February

Out at 4 a.m. due to another raid warning; however, nothing happened. All day today the ship is still burning on the eastern point of the big island which lies due south; must be a tanker which has been beached. Today we heard that the *Empress of Asia*, 10,000 tonnes, was bombed yesterday west of Singapore and had to be beached. She had troops on board who were safely landed without loss of life. Gunfire to the north and east has continued on and off all day.

In Orders this morning, and also in the daily papers, we see published the special Order of the Day from General Wavell, reminding the garrison here that it is like the British Army at the second battle of Ypres; just as that army saved Europe by halting the German advance, so too must we now halt the Japanese advance. He also asks us to emulate the example of the defenders of Tobruk.

My batman has shown me an aeroplane propaganda leaflet he picked up, a picture of a little girl crying and saying, 'Come home, Daddy'.

8 February

Went to General Base Depot by the unit truck to see my friends Alex Reed and Jock White. I found, on arrival, that they had been transferred to the AIF packstore in town. So, the unit truck driver and I drove to the packstore where I met them and, also, Captain MacAlister from Southport. The latter's presence was a complete surprise as I understood he was at Victoria Barracks in Brisbane.

I reached the 13 AGH at 3 p.m. and found the attack on Singapore Island had begun. Numerous ambulances bearing wounded were arriving, so I took my place in the resuscitation ward and the operating theatre. I was on duty until 9 a.m. the next day when I took an hour off to go

*Later Sir David Griffin, Lord Mayor of Sydney.

over to the mess to have breakfast and a brief sleep before again starting work which continued until 10 that night.

In the past 30 hours, with the battle for Singapore Island now beginning, 65 operations were performed at our hospital. The constant pressure of work left one no time to think upon the sorrow and suffering of the unending procession of mangled men filling our resuscitation wards and then taking their turn, one by one, on the operating tables. The resuscitation ward and operating room had to be heavily blanketed at night and, as the night wore on, the crowded rooms became more and more devoid of air. There was not a moment to stop work and throw open the doors and extinguish the light. The atmosphere was hot and humid, a sickly mixture of odours — blood and sweat and antiseptic.

We had now entered upon the black and final stages of this pitiable campaign, which is the darkest day for the British Empire since the collapse of France. It was the beginning of the last week before the final blow — the capitulation.

The weakness of our High Command, the failure of our Air Force, the lack of any strong man to lead either soldiers or the civilian population on the Island, increasing confusion and demoralisation of the troops — all these evils unfolded themselves as one day succeeded another. God bless those brave and cheerful souls from the front who, from time to time, brought renewed confidence and a fighting spirit to the anxious, helpless men in the wards. And God forgive the shivering, jittery wretches who took refuge in the hospital in their dozens, abandoning all their self-respect and their mates to their fates — unsupported — in the firing line.

Sunday, 8 February, was the beginning of the end.
On this day, after a 17-hour barrage, the enemy landed on the west of the Island and, after a week of confused fighting, the capitulation came on the following Sunday, *15th February*. The civilian casualties during the week were 3,000 and these, along with the normal full complement of 1,500, were crowded into Singapore General Hospital.

Monday, 9 February
I left the operating ward about 10 p.m. having been on duty, but for one hour, since 3 p.m. yesterday. I slept well that night and was glad of it because, otherwise, I knew I should not have been able to keep up with my share of the work. We worked more or less in teams, Charles Osborne, Tim Hogg and Eddy in one team, and Bert Navin, Victor Conlon and myself in another. Tom Crankshaw, the specialist and the dentist, gave anaesthetics and helped in the wards.

Outstanding was the tireless energy of some of the sisters. I specially remember a frail-looking little Sister McGlade of Queensland and the help and cheerfulness of the three masseurs, Misses Sutton of Melbourne and Hill and Simpson of Adelaide.

Last, but not least, was the heavy, unending work borne by the stretcher-bearers. One of the most conspicuous was Private Monatt, a beefy muscular youth with a wide grin, apparently tireless, and with the strength of an ox.

By day, the doors of the operating ward were open to admit the sea breezes. By night, we suffocated in the blanketed atmosphere. It was hard in that scene of confusion of littered floors, crammed buckets, splashed plaster of Paris, pools of blood, sweating orderlies with floor mops, prostrate patients gasping or shouting under the anaesthetic, to recognise what had been a peaceful dining room with squared linoleum floors and distant views over sea and islands. But such it had been — our first mess room — when this unit landed in Singapore five short months ago. It was in this same room, now converted to such different usage, that my old friend, Jack Morlet, gave an interesting address one somnolent afternoon on the campaign in 1916-18 in Macedonia.

As well as duties with the operating team, I have to do dressings in the wards. Among my patients, I again find David Griffin and we cheer each other with the latest rumours.

Tuesday, 9 February

A rumour, circulating far and near, told how the Americans had landed and taken Penang. In parts, it was even given out as official. The old proverb will always hold and dishonesty proves a poor policy in the end, even in connection with rumours that are intended to hearten and encourage.

From the topmost of the three floors facing the bay, I can look westward with my glasses toward Singapore Harbour. All seems deserted except for what appear to be one or two burned-out steamers against the wharves. One or more columns of smoke are always rising behind the city. Away to the north the black smoke from the burning naval base is never-ending. For days its black billows in the upper vault of the sky seem to have become solid and motionless, blending into the ever-present blanket of cloud over the city and sweeping with it away to the south-west. To complete the semi-circle of flame and smoke, mid-week our side — a token of approaching collapse — has fired the huge oil-tanks to the south on Dutch Island. From this new conflagration, the whole water of the bay is illuminated at night, rendering unnecessary the beach searchlights which usually scanned sea and sky at night.

Late today when John Rosson was giving an anaesthetic for me, I noticed him take the theatre sister's hand between his own whilst tears came into her eyes. I did not understand this show of emotion at the time, but heard a short time later that the order had come through that all our nursing sisters were to leave us tonight. I heard later that the first batch had gone on the *Wee Sui*, a second batch probably on the *Empire Star*, and a third batch, probably from 10th AGH and English hospitals, on a destroyer.

Sister Margaret Selwood came to say goodbye to me as I was operating in the theatre that night the first batch were to go. We wished each other good luck and, as I turned away to my work, she kissed me on the left cheek. It touched me so much that I felt tears coming to my eyes but I could not say thankyou because she had already flashed out of the room with my message to Barbara in her keeping and I never saw her again. She was always a kind and bright personality, held in warm regard by all. With the second batch of nurses, I sent a scribbled note to Barbara by Sister Bates and I heard she had handed it to Sister Selwood to take to Brisbane, which God grant she may reach safely.

Mid-February 1942

During this fateful week, the smoke by day gave place to lurid flame at night, of which a semi-circle extended from north to west, to the oil tanks on Dutch Island and further yet to the south-east where, on the point of another island, a beached ship burned for many nights and days — evidence of an unlucky tanker destroyed by the oft-appearing Japanese bombers.

Our planes disappeared from the skies. The last I remember seeing was a low-flying Lockheed Hudson bomber which skimmed the hospital roof one evening at dusk and disappeared to the north. The anti-aircraft guns, however, continued to fire by day when the Japanese planes appeared and a couple cracked loudly at intervals. From houses near the neighbouring suburb of Ketong, one morning when I was doing dressings in my ward, there came a loud cheer from some of our men in the quadrangle. One of our shells had upset an enemy plane and everybody was optimistic again at this modest indication of success.

All was confusion and uncertainty after the Japanese landing last Sunday. First, the devastating barrage of artillery and mortar fire during which, according to gunners and infantry, the enemy picked out and plastered with explosives our hidden position with a knowledge and accuracy that was uncanny. Then relays of bombers, 18-28 at a time, would let go their rain of death at one fell swoop. 150 heavy bombs bursting on a small area within a few seconds have a paralysing and shattering effect which cannot be realised by any except those who have experienced it.

It will be understood that, once the enemy had crossed the narrow Straits of Johore and had effected a footing on the Island, then the front line was not far away and the wounded, and often the dead, were brought, so to speak, hot from the firing line. During these fateful days we lost a young medical officer, newly arrived with the last reinforcements. A tall, good-looking, athletic young man with a quiet pleasant manner, he had been in our mess only a few days and I had seen little of him. I was unaware that he had been sent from us for duty at the front where he survived only one day, being brought back to us in the evening, dead. My first knowledge of the tragedy was when, that particular evening, the sergeant major hurried across the quadrangle to me and said, 'Would you come and see Captain Lyndon at once. An ambulance has just brought him in and, although he spoke to me, he is very bad.' I was beside him in the ambulance in a few seconds, but I never heard him speak because he was already dead.

The last night of that fateful week was spent in contemplation — reflecting on my months in Singapore to date, and the reasons behind our swift capitulation to Emperor Hirohito's Army.

Captain R.D. Puflett and Major Harold Park

Medical officers of the 10th Australian General Hospital, Malaya

Sergeant David Griffin

Lieutenant W.G. Barnes (Bill), 1941

Lieutenant R.V. Pockley, 1941

PART THREE

Singapore Sojourn, 1942-45

There is a gap of several months between the Fall of Singapore and the beginning of the diary written in cheap exercise books while Dr Huxtable was in Changi. Presumably he was too busy with the wounded to find time for writing between February and July 1942.

Thursday, 30 July 1942

I had a pleasant walk and talk with Colonel Pigdon in the late afternoon. I never tire of the sight of the tall trees and the glimpses of water over the Straits of Johore. We returned home via the round tower, including the 18th Division area and our playing fields or padang.

Yesterday afternoon Colonel Durham, ADMS, gave a personal address to all our officers. Colonel Summons also spoke of ambulance work and regimental medical officers and I ventured some contrary opinions on advanced dressing stations.

Friday, 31 July

Our afternoon tea at 4.45 p.m. consists of a cup of black tea, without sugar, and a biscuit made of rice flour and often sweetened; rather popular, and a temptation to gatecrashers who occasionally drop in at this time!

It is nice to be hospitable but rations are very limited, so the Messing Officer, Padre Benjamin, has devised a scheme to outwit the uninvited guest. The biscuit plate is left in the kitchen and those of us who belong here walk in and take our own biscuit. Up to date, no gatecrasher has dared venture into the kitchen! The rule of invited guests is that the officer inviting the guest shares his biscuit with him.

We took a flag* and went out over the padang, and on the far side about three-quarters of a mile away, we found a fine swimming bath complete with tiled pavement, springboard, diving tower and dressing sheds, the latter rather cracked and twisted from the nearby bomb bursts. The bath was filled to the brim and looked most inviting except that, having been deserted for all these months since the capitulation, the bottom was covered with dead leaves and other debris.

*The Japanese had ruled that when leaving a compound a flag of identification had to be carried.

We turned and rejoined the bitumen Changi Road that led us back by the 18th Division area; however, before entering the area we visited, in turn, the Australian and British cemeteries which are just beside the road and are well kept.

Our graves have a small concrete cross to each, and on the cross a copper plate bearing no name but just the army number. On the British soldiers' graves are wooden crosses but I'm afraid the weather will efface the carved and painted name that each bears. We saw the grave of Sergeant Brown of the 2/18th battalion who died a few days previously, after losing a leg and many months in bed.

Dick Phillips, Kevin Fagan and Pat O'Donnell from Selarang Barracks are to leave for Japan.

This evening in the cinema we enjoyed a rare treat, a male choir of about 20 voices, trained by an elderly and most efficient officer, visited us from the southern area. They were British troops and I remember a shy young officer, with a pleasant appearance and pleasant but untrained baritone voice singing, amongst other items, 'Oh Star of Eve' by Wagner. The cinema stage boasted a fairly respectable piano and the occasion was, as Colonel Craven said in his speech of thanks at the end of the concert, 'a rare treat'.

Saturday, 1 August
In the afternoon, I walked with Colonel Pigdon to Selarang Barracks and prison area. In the evening some of our officers, usually Frank White, Charles Osborne, Charles Turner, Adrian Farmer, and Cotter Harvey, climb to the top of the old block for the Saturday evening educational address provided by Colonel Craven and officers of A Mess. The lecturer is sometimes an officer belonging to the hospital area and sometimes a visitor from another area. Tonight, it was Major Webster, RAMC, belonging to A Mess itself: he had been several years medical officer in oil companies in Borneo and spoke very interestingly on boring for oil in that country.

Sunday, 2 August
There was parade and church service in the cinema at 10.30 a.m., the sermon given by Major Sandy, the Chaplain. Major Sandy was a Chinese research scholar of Oxford University, for over 20 years in China, and his wife was, or is, a missionary surgeon at Peking Union Medical College. He came to this country as an Army Welfare Officer and then was ordained as a deacon by the Bishop of Singapore. Only recently he became an Army Chaplain. Apparently, the appointment he had from the Bishop of Singapore was purely a nominal one because Sandy, being an Army officer, could not officiate as Deacon of the Cathedral of Singapore. He is probably one of the few English or Europeans who speak and write Mandarin fluently.

Our Sunday Evening Mess talk tonight was given by an Englishman, Captain Maybor, ex-official of Customs of Singapore Island. His talk was on the control of drug traffic at Singapore. A most interesting, indeed exciting, talk of motor launch chases, searching of ships and city premises, underworld feuds and murders. An interesting sideline was that the government allows certain individuals, who can produce a medical certificate to the effect that they are addicted to opium, to have a specified allowance which the Government sells to them: for everyone else, the drug is forbidden.

Colonel Summons, having taken over command of the hospital, has ordered that all officers move up to the top floor of this block. The idea is welcomed as there is more air.

I am continuing with my Japanese studies.

Monday, 3 August

I bought a pineapple at the canteen for 15 cents, normally about 5 pence, one of the few items available nowadays at a fair price. Eggs are 10 cents each, (three-pence halfpenny), Chinese cigarettes are 11 cents for 10.

The Japanese have been giving us, for the past couple of months, what is termed amenities money — not pay, but a kind of pocket money to supplement our rations. It is not ungenerous. Officers receive about $2.50 every ten days: theoretically, we draw $1.75, as the Army keeps the balance to buy extras for the hospital patients. NCOs and men even have their pay docked in proportion. Out of our $1.75, we contribute, by our own private arrangements, 75 cents for the Officers' Mess, so one is left with $1.00 in cash every ten days. This means we can live within our income by spending up to 10 cents a day, a private soldier about 5 cents.

I consider myself lucky, because, some time ago, my good friend Mac contacted someone who changed for me a couple of Australian pounds at the rate of $4 to the pound — good profit for the money-changer, although he will have to wait some time for his profit.

Tuesday, 4 August

Today is the anniversary of the start of the last war, but that is a thing of the past and is not remembered among our present day anxieties and interests. In fact, I believe that last Anzac Day would not have been observed here had it not been for the interest and the activities of a few of us here who still call ourselves returned soldiers. As it was, we had a moving and impressive memorial parade and service which everybody felt touched by and which had a certain, and I hope lasting, effect on our esprit de corps.

At 5 p.m. Captain Markowitz again began his physiology lectures. I forgot to say yesterday that Colonel Julian Taylor is now not going to Japan so we hope for some more lectures in surgery from him. By way of contrast, last night he gave us a talk on Louis XIV of France.

This afternoon I went to Selarang Barracks and had afternoon tea, cocoa and hot water with MacAlister, Jock White and other officers. After the evening meal, I sat on the roof of this building with Cotter Harvey and Campbell Guest, the ex-Red Cross member. We talked about Red Cross activities.

The Red Cross, being an international society, should in my view dispense financial and health aid to war victims in any country, for example, of late years Spain and China. There were 30 million war destitute in China in the early months of the Japanese invasion, yet the total amount of money subscribed by the outside world was about two million pounds, including Red Cross medical supplies, being about one pound and four pence a head to the refugees. MacAlister and White see the Red Cross as a local or patriotic organisation in each country whose obligations and funds afford help to citizens of that particular country only. I experienced this latter view in Queensland in 1938 when trying to arouse interest in the plight of the Chinese in Red Cross circles, and the public through the *Courier Mail* — but there was virtually no response.

Wednesday, 5 August

11 a.m. hurried around to my ward cases, all convalescent, then a swimming excursion to the salt water of the Straits of Johore. The flag party leaves on Wednesday mornings and those lucky enough to know about the departure are eligible to go. Colonel Huston and Major Pemberton, RAMC and Cotter Harvey joined us this morning. First a pleasant walk northward for three-quarters of a mile, much prettier than the walk to Selarang in the other direction, with green slopes, a rocky hill to the left, and flowering trees.

At the southern area gate we turned right and entered that area past where the Sikh sentries are posted,* halfway between the two gates in No Man's Land. The gate at the north end led out on to the large padang or field and then across country and over the grass to the bath situated about half a mile further on.

The scenery is rather lovely. Bougainvillea are in full flower, both the purple and the Thomasia of Queensland; frangipani trees with their fragrant whiteness dotting the green foliage as well as carpeting the ground; yellow cassia and scarlet poinciana often matching their beauty side by side. The padang through which we walk is the same cutting sword grass that we have at home. There is also blue couch grass and a broad blade of grass, half buffalo and half paspalum. This wide padang fronting the streets is, indeed, picturesque, nestling at the foot of the large hill. The surrounding slopes are dotted with buildings, some obviously once-comfortable homes — probably with little English children playing in the garden below — but now alas deserted, and the garden shrubs and trees

---

*A large number of Sikh soldiers deserted to the Japanese.

remain unattended now that their former owners have left and the conquerors are uninterested.

The fenced-in bathing area, about 100 yards long, is a pleasant place with a little sandy beach in front and a springboard and diving tower for when the tide is high. We spent a pleasant hour before gathering together for the march back.

I walked back with Colonel Huston and we talked about the Himalayas. He had lived in India a great deal, his last place being in sight of Nanda Devi, the highest mountain in the Himalayas. He knows Rutledge, Smyth and other famous mountaineers, also Sommerville, the doctor, of the 1922 and 1923 attempts on Everest. A few days after this, Colonel Huston lent me Sommerville's autobiography, *After Everest*. Sommerville settled in india after the second Everest climb at Neyoor Medical Mission in Travencore and did 12 years' work that was, or seemed in the reading thereof, to be superhuman. I much enjoyed the book.

In the evening, Frank Wright and I went to a lecture in the gymnasium (the men's Mess hut) on Christmas Island by an ex-medical officer of the government service there. The island is two days sail south of here and I suppose is now in Japanese hands. Afterwards we did the usual evening stroll around our prison walk and, passing the cinema building, noticed that the AIF concert party, who often visit this hospital, had not yet finished their program. So we got to the doors of the packed building and saw the last few items: I noticed two Japanese officers looking on and apparently enjoying it and bystanders said that at the end, when everyone stood to attention for the National Anthem (which we always sing with much gusto), the Japanese stood to attention also.

Thursday, 6 August

Before sunrise I went, as I often do, to the top of C Mess where sleep Clancy, the American Red Cross man, and Wallace, one of the medical officers, spurning the 'dews of the morning' and even the possibility of an occasional tropical deluge. Here, on the flat roof, it is very pleasant to watch the glories of the sunrise across the eastern end of the Straits while the noises and smells of the hospital area are temporarily surmounted and forgotten. Suddenly, the great golden ball slides above the horizon and, in the glories of the coloured sky, there seem to be rays of hope and promise. The black shape of a junk glides down the channel and, for the moment, is silhouetted in the golden track of sunlight. It seems hard to realise that there is a war going on, except for the constant sorrow of the forced separation and lack of news from home.

Today we heard of the arrival as prisoners at Selarang camp of two Australian sailors and of a British airman who were on a ship that was captured mid-Indian Ocean by the Japanese. We hope for news of home but realise it must be general, about sport, picture shows on Sundays and the Americans, not about personal things for which each one of us is waiting.

Saturday, 15 August

In the afternoon, all officers from here were sent to Selarang. It only takes about 20 minutes to march across. About two or three hundred officers of all units, except those working in Singapore, were assembled on the ground floor of the big block where, in the early days, was situated the 10th Australian General Hospital before we amalgamated. The occasion was the farewell to the GOC General Callaghan, who is going with all the other senior officers — colonels and upwards — to Japan. His successor Lieutenant-Colonel Galleghan (Black Jack of the 30th Battalion), took the chair. The speeches were sincere and inspiring. Lieutenant-Colonels Kappe and Thyer spoke after Galleghan. Then the GOC replied with feeling, as also did Brigadier Maxwell. The latter is a medical man in practice in Cootamundra, N.S.W. Shortly after this he contracted dysentery and was unable to leave with the others for Japan. He therefore joined our staff at the hospital, and a most fortunate acquisition he was.

After the meeting I said good-bye again to Colonel Pigdon. It is with rather a heavy heart that I see him go.

Sunday, 16 August

Many cars and trucks passed through, taking the party away to the ships for Japan; some hundreds of troops are reported to be going as well. Where are they going to and for how long? What is to be their ultimate fate?

Saturday, 22 August

We now have electric light throughout the hospital. Also the luxury of fans. The nights are now cheerful and interesting, instead of recurring periods of gloom and depression with nothing to do but walk up and down the bitumen road like a caged animal, or to sit and yarn on a hot concrete verandah.

Another windfall during August has been the news that Red Cross circles in South Africa had shipped to us some maize flour, jam and caramels. The maize flour makes a change from rice for a breakfast dish. The jam, particularly, is most acceptable. The caramels, of which we each received 17 to 19, were 'doctored' with ingredients which the kindly South Africans considered good for us. Mine tasted of cod-liver oil. It is not only the extra food which is welcome, but also the knowledge that, at last, a contact has been made with the outside world and there is hope that, by the same means, our postcards may by now have reached Australia.

In the afternoon, I went to Selarang with Frank Wright to see Jock White and MacAlister. Mac, of course, produced cocoa to drink. The old brigade of Diggers were all there — Morrison, Cribb and the others.

After late tea, I went to A Mess and heard a young Londoner give an address on journalism.

Sunday, 23 August

Jock White came over to our evening meal at my invitation. We had a little meat ration and I gave him, to finish up with, a nice fresh pineapple. We played billiards for a short time afterwards and about 10 p.m. Frank Wright and I took a flag and escorted Jock out of our gate and across No-Man's Land to the Selarang North Gate. The Sikh sentries are not on duty at night and we were hoping that we would not run into a Japanese bicycle patrol, in which case we might have been stopped and questioned in spite of carrying a pass flag. However, we arrived back without incident.

Monday, 24 August

A man recently died in our surgical ward from a spreading gangrene of the skin of the scrotum. At first it was thought to be a spreading gangrenous dermatitis of streptococcul type, but later the pathologists decided it was a diphtheric infection. This fits in with an epidemic of throat and nasal diphtheria which has broken out amongst working parties in Singapore, and which has given rise to anxiety owing to the shortage of anti-toxin. The hospitals (British and AGH) unfortunately don't carry stocks and the Japanese authorities will only let us have limited supplies.

Lately it has been found that several cases of scrotal dermatitis, also ordinary-looking tropical ulcers on the body, have shown the presence of a super-added infection with a diphtheria bacillus. For months past, both patients and personnel have been troubled by this scrotal dermatitis. It has been a veritable epidemic and in most cases appears to break out with itchiness and soreness in men who do not give any preceding history of tinea or dhobi itch. The soldiers have an amusing name for this condition which they put down to the diet of rice, and they may be right, and that is a form of avitaminosis.

Personally I think that the skin irritation is probably due, in part at least, to the chemical irritation of moisture, dirt and the crude yellow Chinese soap which is issued to all prisoners of war. Most men have one, sometimes two, showers a day — even those in the Singapore working parties (of whom there are about 8,000 AIF). This would be all to the good if they had good toilet soap and a clean dry towel and powder to finish up. The towels alone are an offence to the skin, being dirty, damp rags of cloth.

Tuesday, 25 August

Adrian Farmer, ENT specialist from Melbourne, and I have been put in charge of part of the hospital that has been set aside for: all Australians with diphtheria of the throat or nose; and all men, British and Australian, who have diphtheritic skin lesions. I am in charge of the latter and welcome the idea of having Tommies, once again, as patients.

Wednesday, 26 August

This is swimming day, but no time now. Our department consists of two rooms at the far south-eastern corner of the hospital on the ground floor of the last block of buildings and on the far side of the block, i.e., looking out on to the barbed wire. Each room will hold 26 at a pinch and consists of a rectangular concrete chamber open on one side, with a row of doors which open outwards on to a concrete verandah. There is no ventilation in the roof but there are now two large fans in each room which are now working. Then there is also a dark and rather uninviting atap hut just opposite across a small plot of grass into which we can overflow when the wards are full. There is one outside shower over a concrete drain in the open air and a running water tap. And one water closet for our possible 80 patients. It is to be hoped it is in working order and will remain so, otherwise there is a walk of some distance to the outside latrines.

My spirit failed at first sight of the bare, unfurnished and rather dirty premises, nothing to write on, sit on or any table to put things on, no stationery, no cupboards for the men, nothing for their bedside requirements (mugs, brushes, etc.) except to put them on the floor under the beds. it reminds me of the dysentery wards last March when we first arrived here, and I was put in charge of a whole half floor (70 beds) of dysentery cases in a space that would only hold 40 to 50 with any comfort. Ward utensils and requisites were mixed up and lying everywhere about the hospital in those chaotic days just following our move here. Reg Wright and I had to 'scrounge' personally anything we required for our 140 sick men. But in those days the morale was low and what discouraged and often disgusted me was the piracy that went on between one ward and another. For instance, after a great deal of trouble and searching one would at last acquire, say, a hypodermic syringe or a pair of scissors. The next day, when one urgently required the same for some patient, one would find it had disappeared, 'lifted' by someone from another ward never to return. There was a great deal of hard, conscientious work done in those days by orderlies and medical officers alike, but there was also a great deal of self-pity, loafing and shirking (passing the buck as it is called in the Army), a kind of demoralisation that set in after the surrender. Colonel Pigdon fought it hard and he had all my admiration for his constant and untiring efforts. Well, now at any rate, we have trained and willing orderlies and two good sergeants — Sergeant Street, morning shift, and Sergeant Pearson, afternoon shift. I am also lucky as having as my chief dressers Privates Albert Freeman of the Ninth Field Ambulance (who was postman and occasional preacher at Sunday Services at Kota Tinggi) and Ward who works in the atap hut.

Thursday, 27 August

The afternoon address was given by Major Bruce Anderson who has been around Mersing for the last two months and, being out of touch with us here, there has been some anxiety for him and the working party of AIF engineers with whom he was acting as medical officer. This party was sent north to the east coast at Mersing, being employed by the Japanese in removing the land-mines which had been placed there as part of our defences last year. This can be a dangerous job and there was one accident in which a couple of our men were killed and others injured.

In the evening I had to dress many new cases admitted to my ward and so missed a lecture I would like to have heard which was given by an Australian sailor recently captured.

Friday, 28 August

Pleasant and fresh after the rains. Received a letter from Dick Pockley and a toothbrush as a gift from that generous soul. I already have a couple in reserve, I don't think I will use it as it is of Chinese make. He reminds me in the accompanying note that, in the early days of the capitulation, I gave him one! He shows signs of fed-upness but his cheeriness appears to prevail, and he tells me that he, Captain Dave Hinder, Captain Hendry, and Major Carter have produced a one-act play.

My impression of the causes of the skin cases which are flooding my ward remains the same, that of lack of hygiene; work, sweat, dirty clothes and dirty towels, and the crude, caustic soap.

Tonight I had hoped to take Bill Barnes,* with the help of Jack Fuller, to the Windmill Theatre. I had arranged to get a wheelchair for him. I walked with a flag party across to the Eighteenth Division area and saw Major Wood in charge of the box-office but he can't give us seats for tonight. A good variety show with Denis East and George Wall providing the highlights. Wood said to come tomorrow or Monday.

On the walk back I had to go alone with the flag as there happened to be no flag party. The Sikh sentry held me up half way and intimated by signs and a nasty look on his face that I had not saluted him properly. As one of our officers recently was struck on the face and jaw several times by one of these men, I listened to what he had to say, then asked permission to proceed, which he agreed to with a grunt.

Sunday, 30 August

8.30 a.m. Holy Communion (Padre Pain of Ballarat) in the cinema. Walked back afterwards with John Oakeshott of Lismore. Busy all day in the diphtheria ward. This afternoon Colonel Craven addressed all officers in the cinema on the question of signing a declaration form produced by the Imperial Japanese Army which required each of us to give his pledge not to attempt to escape under any circumstances. A great deal of interest and excitement is aroused.

Monday, 31 August

Had arranged to go to the Windmill Theatre tonight with Bill Barnes and Jack Fuller, but in the evening I found that all leave had been cancelled, i.e. no permission to leave our own area, so had to call our party off yet again.

August has been a good month. It has seen the coming of the electric light to the hospital with a consequent brightening and cheering influence both on the patients and staff. Also the fans are a comfort on hot nights, especially in some of the less ventilated rooms used as wards.

Another feature of August has been the contact made with the outside world in that South Africa has been able to send us one lot of Red Cross supplies. No sign of any repetition, unfortunately, but it has given us reason to hope.

Tuesday, 1 September

A grand muster parade is ordered for today by the Japanese so everyone in the hospital area is up at 7.15 a.m. After breakfast we fell in at 8.30 a.m. in the space between two of the hospital buildings — between N Block and O Block. Officers all at one end — 28 of us (30 counting Colonel Summons and Major Cade who were racing around with the Japanese authorities).

At first, all heads were counted at least three times by Japanese soldiers and officers. We saw sedan cars then drive along the road and one or two parties of senior Japanese officers walked about. Having counted the personnel, different parties entered the wards (one of our officers was on duty in each) and counted the patients and the staff there.

Meanwhile we stood on parade or, alternately, sat on the ground from 8.30 a.m. to 1.45 p.m. Japanese soldiers were posted as sentries along our flanks. I had a long talk with Brigadier Maxwell of Cootamundra who told me his weight was down six stone, from 17 stone to 11. He is 6'4" tall.

Wednesday, 2 September

In the morning an urgent 'return' was called for from each ward, requiring the number of patients who could walk two miles, those who could walk 100 yards and those who could not walk at all; it looked like a big upheaval. Later we heard that the hospital was not to be moved, but that all personnel, British and Australian, were to go at once to Selarang Barrack Square. Soon the big trek had begun. There was a ceaseless procession through the hospital area all the afternoon because all troops and details from the southern area and from the Malayan Command area pass through here. It looked like what one imagined the war refugees in France and Belgium looked like, except there were no women and children — just men in all kinds of clothes, military and naval, rags and tatters, all most pathetic. *

Nearly a mile to the east of us we could see a parallel procession moving along the Changi Road to Selarang — that was the 18th British Division. Officers and men alike humped their own possessions and the loads were all heavy. It looked as if they were going for good, so each man took all he could carry and, for most, it was a weary two miles or more along the bitumen with three long steep hills.

The improvised vehicles were ingenious. Many of the men carried shoulder poles like Chinese coolies; most pulled or dragged things; some had wheels of different sizes fixed on to things such as army stretchers which were pulled along the ground, or box-carts or improvised trailers, wheelbarrows, etc. One tall Englishman had a complete iron bedstead strapped to his back and he walked along erect and even brisk, looking a comical sight from behind from which aspect one could only see an upright bed moving along with packs and parcels strapped underneath it. Two men dragged a piece of wire netting with all their belongings on it. Some bodies of troops marched as units carrying their packs and singing or whistling as they swung along.

By late that afternoon, all had passed through. Colonel Craven, Commanding Officer of this hospital area, spoke to a parade of our Australian Section, telling us of the decision by the Japanese authorities that all prisoners of war were to move to the Selarang camp area. He also told us that he, and other senior officers, had witnessed the execution of four of our soldiers, two British and two Australian, who had attempted to escape.

Friday, 4 September
We can see that tents and marquees have been erected on the roofs of Selarang in an attempt to house everyone.

It is announced that until we sign the 'no escape' document we will all have half rations, eight ounces of rice a day. We are shut off from the outside world with no discharges from hospital and no admissions, except one or two odd trucks have been allowed in from Singapore with sick men.

On Friday night we heard that the unequal contest is over, and that an arrangement has been made whereby each officer, NCO and man has to sign the declaration which the Japanese authorities require. We have been ordered by our own military authorities to sign tonight and the papers are being distributed to all patients and other personnel.

*This became known as the Selarang Barrack Square Incident. On 30 August 1942 all area commanders were ordered to arrange that all personnel signed the following undertaking: 'I, the undersigned, hereby solemnly swear on my honour that I will not, under any circumstances, attempt to escape'. The Japanese demanded this because two British and two Australian soldiers had been caught when attempting to escape from Changi. They were executed in the presence of all area commanders on 2 September 1942.

The area commanders refused to sign this on principle. So all British and Australian troops were ordered to Selarang Barracks where an area usually limited to 800 people, even then with less than adequate sanitary facilities, was expected to cope with 13,350 British and 2,050 Australians. Despite the best endeavours to provide sanitary facilities, within a short period of time more than 1,000 were seriously ill with dysentery and diphtheria. Then the Japanese threatened to reduce rations by 50 per cent. Malaya command gave in and by 5 September 1942 all declarations were completed and troops allowed to return to previous quarters.

Officers had to go to the Orderly Room to sign but when my turn came they had run out of papers so I had to go up to the English Orderly Room to obtain one.

Saturday, 5 September

The troops are returning from Selarang to their original quarters in the surrounding countryside. All are unwashed and tired, many limping along and all, as before, are overloaded. Some of the trailers, pulled by 15 to 20 men, are a weird sight piled with stoves, packs, beds, lamps, chairs and fowl crates. About a dozen of our orderlies who are off duty turned to, like the good Samaritans that they are, and gave their help to those who needed it most up this rather steep hill. I watched these lads work for a couple of hours and tried to get others to help and lent a hand myself. An elderly and tired-looking officer limped along. He had a grizzled moustache and looked like a regular soldier which he turned out to be. He had a suitcase on one arm, a load on his back and a fox terrier and a hurricane lamp in his left hand. I offered to help and he thanked me and suggested that I take the dog chain and the hurricane lamp with the explanation, 'I can then use my stick. I had a broken leg and am not long out of hospital.' Along the couple of hundred yards walk through the hospital grounds I learned that he was Colonel Swinton of the Second East Surreys. He knew Victor Hawkins slightly and Harris, amongst others, of the Lancaster Fusiliers whom I knew. Harris was a Lieutenant in the last war but in this war he took the battalion to France as their colonel. Colonel Swinton and I parted at the gate, a nice man and I hope we meet again.

Sunday, 6 September

Colonel Galleghan, known as 'Black Jack', now in command of the AIF prisoners in Malaya, visited the hospital this afternoon and addressed the hospital personnel (Australian side) in the gymnasium (Mess room). He spoke forcefully as he described the course of the negotiations with the Japanese authorities which resulted in the signing of the forms. Colonel Galleghan looks every inch the soldier, is always correctly turned out, and has the reputation of a good battalion commander.

Note: Mess arrangements:

The hospital orderlies and outside workers of whom we have almost 420 on the Australian side, have their meals in two sittings. There are now tables and benches.

Each man brings a plate or a mess tin and his spoon, and mug. Each gives his messing number to the sergeant on duty and is ticked off on the sergeant's list as he walks past to the serving table where he gets his ladleful of rice (sometimes two ladles) and a ladle of sauce, coconut or stew (the latter about three times a week) over the rice from the next server. If there is bread for the meal, mostly once a day but sometimes twice, it is lying in cut pieces and he picks up his one piece, about three inches by three inches and three-quarters of an inch thick. The tea is black with no sugar. At breakfast he gets a porridge made of brown or baked rice and either a ladleful of very watery condensed milk or, until recently, a dessertspoon full of sugar instead.

On the whole, the food is not too bad and there is plenty of rice to fill up with so that nobody need feel empty. The jam from the South African Red Cross appears to be finished. It was, while it lasted, being issued one dessertspoonful for each man with his rice, once a day.

The ticking off of names and numbers on a list at meal times is to prevent double banking, i.e. some of the 'clever ones' used to gobble up a first helping and then fall in at the end of the line again and get a second meal.

Thus ends the week of the 'black hole of Selarang'. Those who were in it for the three days came through unscathed, with very few exceptions. All showed a good spirit of cheerfulness. It has done a great deal to promote a feeling of brotherhood between British and AIF soldiers, thus removing the feeling of prejudice and antipathy that has existed between the two forces, principally on our side, and which has been deliberately fanned and kept alive by several people, not least some officers. In the last war this pettiness and insularity were to be found amongst medical rather than amongst combatant officers, and so it is in this war. Combatants have a broader, more manly and less selfish outlook.

Our senior (AIF) combatant officers have often shown themselves to be aware of the existence of this failing in the AIF and have worked for 'entente cordiale' — I have noticed this in the speeches of such men as our late GOC, General Callaghan, our brigadiers and also Lieutenant Colonel Kappe and our present Commander, Colonel Galleghan.

Personally, my conscience has given me no qualms over the signing of the papers.

Wednesday, 7 September

The 'flag ferry services' are again operating between the various prison areas. This afternoon, accordingly, I walked across to Selarang to see Jock White and MacAlister; the latter was away with Captain Gunther on sanitation work, chiefly filling in latrines that had been dug in the barrack square to accommodate last week's concentration of the 15,000 troops. The stench still rises and pervades the whole area of the barracks, which measures 108 paces across and 227 paces in length, and this provides space of about 24,516 square yds.

Surrounding the square on three sides there are the seven buildings each with the ground floor and two upper floors and, of course, the flat roof. When in February and March last, we used two of these buildings as our hospital, we had each floor crammed to capacity with beds touching and, under those conditions, each floor would take 140 patients — i.e.

420 to a building. Supposing that, with well men without beds, we crowded another 40 on to each floor to sleep, this would mean 540 men to a building. The seven buildings, thus packed to the limit, would take, say, 3,780 — this including verandah space. With approximately 3,500 men occupying the buildings, this still leaves 12,000 to be fitted into the barrack square, i.e. there was living space for all purposes, including latrine space and kitchen space, of two square yards per man.

On looking at the barrack square with its blackened, scarred buildings, I found it hard to believe it was the same square which I had first seen last October before the war when it was occupied by the 2nd Gordon Highlanders. The buildings then were grey and clean, the square was empty except for a solitary piper who stood in the centre for a few minutes and played a call to indicate a time on the clock or perhaps a meal. An Indian shop occupied one of the ground floors and here sat tailors on the floor making shorts or shirts or other requisites for the troops. One old man with a beard and glasses sewed a neat puggaree around my Australian hat while I waited. A little English boy aged about eight chatted with me while we looked at magazines at a paper stall. Wives wheeling perambulators went past in the distance, heading towards the padang where there was to be a football match, Gordons versus Argyles.

But now! A shut-in area of gloomy buildings daubed with black paint, blasted by the bombers who did not have to come at night but flew across at will in daylight. An upheaval of red earthworks replacing the bitumen over about a third of the square, the recently dug latrines now being filled in. The Gordons, with depleted ranks, are still in the neighbourhood, but where are now the white wives and little children? For the fortunate, perhaps safely in Colombo or Australia, but many of them missed the last boat.

Saturday, 10 September
In the evening to the Windmill Theatre in the 18th Division area, only ten minutes walk from here. I was accompanied by Carl Furner and Bill Barnes who is now quite proficient on his crutches and can bear a certain amount of weight on his wounded left ankle. We took a wheelchair in case he became tired — Carl Furner helped me push him. A tall, fair young man dressed in full evening dress with white tie and tails (where did he get his clothes?) was very clever with a pack of cards and he entertained and mystified the audience with various tricks. There was an orchestra and the instruments included a fiddle, ukuleles and the entire outfit was made here in the prison camp. A miniature Tommy Atkins with a comical face was an expert with the handbones.

Sunday, 13 September
This afternoon there was a pilgrimage to the AIF cemetery — a little plot of ground in a clearing beside the Changi Road, about a mile east of here, but hidden from the road by trees.

The event was organised by the Malayan Ex-Servicemen's Association, a branch of the Returned Soldiers' League which has been formed here recently by some old diggers. Those of us attending from the hospital area fell in on parade just after the midday meal, in two sections — past war men wearing ribbons in front, junior members in rear — about 15 of each. Bruce Hunt took the parade. He and I marched in front, and Padre Jones at the back, to the Convalescent Depot building at Selarang. We were joined here by about 150 others and marched out along the Changi Road. We formed a hollow square around the area — Colonel Galleghan gave an address and we sang some hymns. The Padre in charge read 'They shall not grow old'. A red wreath was placed in the centre, the bugler played the Last Post and then Reveille. We then marched back, past Colonel Galleghan who took the salute from the roadside.

Monday, 14 September
We were granted an allowance of tobacco today for the coming week, it should last longer than the usual packet of ten cigarettes. Padre Pain has shown me how to roll a cigarette, a feat I was too lazy to learn before: it is rather fascinating.

In the evening I went to see some moving pictures, our first experience! There is a small set doing the rounds of the hospital, property of the 18th Division. Those in the starring roles were Harold Lloyd and Daphne Pollard, my old favourite of the last war in London.

Friday, 18 September
Am Orderly Officer today so was up at Reveille. The rice is cooked much better at the men's meals. I told the cook last week what I thought of the mushy stuff he served up!

This afternoon the Changi Medical Society had a meeting in the cinema — very interesting cases were shown, specially four cases of paralysis of the legs (spastic paraplegia) from the English wards, due to some unknown avitaminosis. Also, a case of pellagra with extensive skin rash.

Lieutenant Colonel Glynn White came to our quarters afterwards, as usual, excited about the news he was bringing: namely that some prisoners have been brought to this area who had been taken in Batavia and possibly some who had been taken in Timor. We are most anxious to hear their news.

Sunday, 20 September
Major Farmer not well, swollen legs, so I had to look after all the diphtheria cases today. However, the throat cases are all convalescent and the ward half empty. My skin cases are doing well.

I went to 8.30 a.m. Holy Communion today in the cinema. Three wounded lads from the Officers' ward were there, too: Bill Barnes, Dolamore of Melbourne, and Bob Sneddon being all leg cases (Sneddon — amputation at the thigh). They stood in a row at the edge of the stage to receive the sacrament, whilst the rest of those present went on to the stage in front of the altar.

At 7.30 p.m., all personnel went to Church Parade in the cinema. The new Officer Commanding, Colonel Galleghan, ordered units to have their Church Parade in the evenings instead of the mornings.

Yesterday afternoon we were warned to be in our wards from 3.30 p.m. onwards as a senior Japanese medico was to visit us. I doubted from past experience whether he would turn up so I took a book and sat under the trees in a pleasant grassy grove which adjoins my ward. There were birds overhead, and a couple of squirrels amused me for a time. The local squirrel is rather sleek and long and his tail is not very bushy. He holds it straight out, not curled, and is continually flicking it. Coloured like a rat but with gold brown under the body, he has a longitudinal black-and-white stripe on each flank. One was feeding on the inner part of the flowers growing high up on a tree and was tearing the flowers to pieces and throwing down the petals in a most wasteful manner. The other did a balancing act on a coconut palm frond, climbing right out to the end of a downward-bending frond and hanging upside down by one foot only, and then recovering his position without the slightest trouble.

On Saturday evening after the meal I took a young man called Lodge up to A Mess and there we listened to a talk on Spanish bullfighting by an English Officer who had at one time lived in Spain. Colonel Craven gave his usual address of thanks, we all know well now how it will begin: first a rather mellow cough to clear the throat, then 'Well, gentlemen, I'm sure you will agree with me, etc. etc.'

This afternoon was marked by an event of great interest to me. Ian Perry, of Brisbane, walked in to see Bernard Clark and possibly me also — he had heard we were both here. Ian had just arrived here from Timor via Batavia, six weeks en route. At Batavia he saw Brian Fihally, RAAF — a POW there now. Young Fihally was in Nugent Walsh's flight in Brisbane early last year. I remember taking them both to lunch at the Cecil Hotel one weekend when they were in Southport. They were expecting to go overseas at any time, then. They were a fine pair of young officers. Ian thinks that Nugent is still in the Middle East. I do hope he is all right. Fihally was sent either to Sumatra or Java from the Middle East when the fighting was in progress in Malaya. He was shot down into the sea, according to Perry, and narrowly escaped with his life.

Monday, 21 September

Today was memorable in that my friend Bill Barnes left hospital after nearly eight months there. I kept in touch with him all that time and watched his progress. At first it seemed he might lose his foot from his shattered left leg; however, it eventually united but the bone has some forward bowing and movements of ankle are very limited. Most of the big tendon had been shot away. He is a fine young man with lots of guts like his mates Alan McClean, Bob Seddon and Jack Fuller. The two former are still in ward with unhealed thigh stumps. Jack Fuller, the ex-medical student, is still in our Mess and studying hard. But Bill Barnes will never again shine at football, his favourite game. Captain Dolamore, 'the Count', will go with him to the Convalescent Depot on Wednesday.

Tonight we had a farewell theatre party over to the Windmill Theatre. Carl Furner helped me and we took the three wounded officers with us — not strict hospital rules but we 'made it', taking our time to cover the half-mile distance, Dolamore in a wheelchair, the others managing on crutches. The theatre troupe put on a very good play which now runs nightly: *I Killed the Count*. The 200 to 300 Tommies present were very appreciative of the thrills and also the laughs. The Inspector from Scotland Yard was especially good, a short brisk man with a barking voice, Captain Wilkinson. He played Leonard in *The Dover Road* in which, poor man, he wore a thick English tweed suit, slightly too large for him, with a waistcoat. The climate being what it is, I admired his stamina.

Sunday, 27 September
Whilst at tea, prior to Church, I had to proceed apace to one of the wards to meet the unexpected arrival of a party of Japanese, two officers and a private. Cotter Harvey was present and, together, we showed them two wards. Cotter went into detail about certain cases but his efforts were wasted because, before shaking hands and stepping into their car, the senior officer revealed that they were not doctors. We are still unaware of the purpose of their visit.

Tuesday, 29 September
Heard of a concert in English Officers' ward so went up (this was about 3 p.m.) and sat beside Phillips who is still a patient there. Dennis East and Coles played violin and accordian. George Wall and Aubrey King sang. Fowler and one other masqueraded in women's clothes, a delightful skit.

Afterwards, East told me about a concert tonight over at Selarang, so at 7 p.m. I met the Windmill Theatre troupe at our gate and marched with them to Selarang. Padre Haig led us and there were about 50 present, including the choir and a few hangers-on. The concert was held in the very pleasant hall, with platform, at the Convalescent Depot, and I sat next to Major Claffy (eye specialist), Alan Rogers, Kevin Fagan and MacAlister. Dennis East played a Mendelsohn concerto that lasted about 25 minutes. When I asked him on the way home how they had the music for the piano accompaniment he told me that he had written the whole arrangement from gramophone records which they had managed to obtain during their imprisonment!

Wednesday, 30 September
Today started with the grim reminder that I had entered my 52nd year! My only regret has been the time being spent away from home and so

wasted as regards most of my desires and some of my duties. While the war lasts, I still wish to be among those of our men who are bearing the brunt, and helping them. However, in our position here, the wounded still with us are now almost healed for the most part. Many are sick but for each of the medical officers there are only a couple of hours' work each day. In one's sixth decade, time has become very precious. There is the haunting thought of those at home with no news from us, and of course, there is no news for us from them. There is the reassuring thought that America is helping to keep them safe but no reassurance about the personal things that mean so much.

I went to Holy Communion at 8.30 a.m. with my friend Padre Pain. The little chapel in the basement of one of the English buildings is very restful. Although there are little blue cushions to kneel on, the concrete floor is hard. On one of the walls an artist among the English soldiers* is drawing a life-size scene of the Nativity in coloured chalks. Preparing for Christmas already!

This evening we had to write nominal rolls of ourselves and patients for the Imperial Japanese Army. Details of age, address, peacetime occupation, parents' addresses, etc. To what purpose, no one knows.

About 10 p.m., before we turned in, kind old Geoff Davies asked me to have supper and presented me with a tin of pineapple for my birthday. We opened it and devoured it together!

Thursday, 1 October

Geoff Davies and I took a flag at 6.15 p.m. and proceeded to the southern area via 18th Division area. At the gate we met Dennis East by arrangement and walked with him to Changi Village to the concert which is held there every evening in the open-air theatre. Branches hang overhead and it is a pleasant place in the cool of the evening. On stage there is a really good choir of officers and men trained and conducted by Captain McNeish. The young soloist, an officer by the name of Ian McLaren about 20 years of age, has a rich baritone voice. Their best items were 'Swing Low Sweet Chariot' and the 'Heavens Resound' (Beethoven and orchestra). The orchestra played 'Invitation to the Waltz', 'March Militaire' and were to have played excerpts from 'Die Fledermaus' but rain began to fall and we had to disperse. Dennis East led the three fiddles and also played a solo during the rain. He supplied and made up all the music for the pianist, he never uses any. He is a member of the Boyd Neil Orchestra in London as well as the Queen's Hall Orchestra. He mentioned that, by a curious coincidence, two fellow students from the Royal Academy of Music in London are prisoners here with him — George Wall, the singer, and young Cliff, anti-aircraft unit. They all came out to Malaya in different units unknown to each other.

---

*The artist was the young Ronald Searle, later a celebrated cartoonist and illustrator.

Recently Japanese troops, obviously recruits, have been marching through our hospital grounds daily to rifle and machine-gun practice on some shooting range over by Selarang. They return in the evenings. Then, on a recent weekend, they practised with 2-inch trench mortars all one afternoon on the level ground between here and Selarang where our men play football. Black bursts exploded every few minutes most of the afternoon, in the middle of our playing field, and the air was rent with ear-splitting explosions. However, subsequently it was found that the craters were very shallow and did not mar the ground for football.

Saturday, 3 October
A windfall today! Red Cross stores have arrived via India, sent once again by the South African Red Cross. Earlier today a pyramid of cases of tinned milk was dumped inside hospital gates. They had been brought up the Straits to the wharf at Fairy Point and then pushed along the rail track by hand on one of the old trucks. All afternoon, trailer parties of the hospital staff had pulled the cases up the slope and round to the Red Cross store. The troops were told by Mr Roberts of the Red Cross that it was food intended for all, not only for the sick.

Because there was no proper supervision provided by either the British Orderly Room or by ours, a few dozen cases 'disappeared'. This led to searches of the men's quarters the next day and to angry reprisals by the authorities, some men getting 28 days in detention barracks over at Selarang. Possibly those caught and punished were passive rather than active participants in the looting. Anyway, some of us felt that the main fault lay in the lack of supervision and organisation, a common fault of the hospitals.

Sunday, 4 October
Church Parade in the gymnasium was marred by talking, chiefly because those at the back could not hear due to the bad acoustics of the hall and Padre Jones' Welsh accent blended with the noise of the sparrows! Colonel Summons spoke sharply about it at the end of the Parade and ordered the unhappy Orderly Officer (Jack Fuller) to take names.

Tuesday, 6 October
I managed to arrange for a display of moving pictures by the hospital outfit for my diphtheria ward on the grass outside. The Tommies on the two top floors turned out and looked on by leaning over their balconies. The films were silent ones, of course, and rather ancient, but much appreciated.

Thursday, 8 October
Whilst passing our Admission and Discharge room, I saw two unkempt Australian soldiers and stopped to talk to them. They had left Java last Saturday, arriving Singapore yesterday. One belonged to the 2/3rd

Machine Gun Battalion sent from the Middle East only to be captured in Java, poor fellows! The other belonged to the 2/3rd Motor Transport Company who left Singapore too late and were all captured with vehicles in Java.

Today I talked with Bob Douglas of Mungallala who told me Jim Crombie is all right and with a working party in Singapore. I last saw Jim here eight months ago, a week after the surrender. I also had a long talk with Sid Bignell of Upper Coomera. Both Bignell and Douglas are very thin and rather anaemic, with sore feet, etc. I asked Frew and Hunt, their MOs, to look after them.

Today I have orders to report for duty at Selarang to second Convalescent Depot. My batman Thomas had my things packed and, at 5 p.m., having said goodbye to staff and patients, I set off by ambulance car in company with Robin Orr (and all his eye apparatus) and Horace Tucker. We reported to Colonel Webster, MC, on arrival: at the same building where we all spent our first miserable night after saying goodbye to Singapore and freedom and arriving at Changi last February as POWs.

Friday, 9 October

I have been glad to leave in some ways; sorry in others. I have been told by Colonel Summons that it is a temporary exchange of officers. Captain C.R. Boyce of Queensland has replaced me. A change from so long at the hospital is good, and over here there is greater space, more air and a greater variety of people to meet. However, I miss the patients and the morning work in the wards. My diptheria skin cases have all been doing well and I was enjoying having Tommies to look after, as well as our own fellows. My ward staff, including Sergeants Lockwood and Pearson and Privates Ward, Albert Freeman (the Methodist Minister), Barber, Cahill, Ryan and even the rough farmers Schlieb and Swan were all good fellows and worked harmoniously. Major Graves and Captain Brown of the British side were very pleasant to be associated with. The NCO in charge of the British dispensary, however, was inclined to be disobliging and to imagine, as men in such positions often do in the Army, that they are still in civilian life, and therefore are endowed with all the importance and independence of a non-combatant civilian.

Over here, at the so-called Convalescent Depot, we have about 250 patients and about 200 staff. Lieutenant-Colonel Webster is in command with Lieutenant-Colonel Leggatt (late of 40th Battallion — Timor) as 2 i/c and Lieutenant Farndon as Adjutant. Lieutenant Alan Carrick, also from Timor and originally from Sydney, is one of the other administrative officers with Lieutenant Male of AIC being the third. Fred Anderson (2/15th Field Regiment) is coming in as QM, to give Captain Patterson, the former quartermaster, a change.

My charge is that section which comprises all convalescent medical cases and is housed in the most north-easterly of the seven large building blocks in the famous square. The old Officers' Mess of the former garrison battalion houses all the convalescent surgical cases, about 150. They come under Colonel Webster and Captain Smith.

Other officers attached are Major Buerkner, physical training, Padre McNeil and Mr Ivor Hangar and McNeilly (YMCA representative) and Captain Greener, formerly 18th Division staff as Educational Officer. He has Sergeants David Griffin and Kelynack with him at the Education Centre, which consists of a couple of rooms at one end of the big surgical building mentioned above.

The library is far from extensive but there are a few educational books and numerous lectures are arranged and various classes, chiefly language classes. I plan to continue the Japanese classes here with Lieutenant Waite, which I was taking at the hospital twice a week.

Occupational and trade technical training have not been instituted in the POW camps here, which seems a pity, but difficulties are presented by the shortage or absence of tools and material, and also by the constant moving of parties of troops into Singapore (Syonan, as they call it) by the Japanese for working camps.

Saturday, 10 October
I forgot to say that one of my diphtheria patients in S1 block was an English private soldier of the Norfolk Regiment named Beer — a comforting reminiscent name these days — and this lad lives in the precincts of the mental hospital at Thorpe at Norwich. His father is a warder in that hospital which is the place where I was attached in July and August of 1918 in the days when it was a big war hospital. These days, he tells me, only half of it is being used as a war hospital. I have been told by many of the Tommies that their fathers served in the last war, not a few of them having been killed in action.

Sunday, 11 October
The Church Parade at 7.30 p.m. was taken by Padre Barrett. I sat next to Bill Barnes and Dolamore. The singing is most inspiring at these Services. I have never heard in peacetime such full-throated singing of 'God Save the King'. Why is it in peacetime we become apathetic, or even diffident about our traditions, and our attitude towards the great Commonwealth of English-speaking countries to which we belong? After the service we sat out on the lawn overlooking the distant Straits of Johore with the hospital lights twinkling a mile away to the right in the middle distance. Inside the piano was going and the convalescents were joining in community songs.

We had some black tea in Bill Barnes' room and there I met Lieutenant Eales of the 2/26th Battalion (he married Helen Craig of Brisbane).

All this afternoon I watched a cricket match across the road on the padang belonging to the 11th English Division. English versus Australia. The latter won, partly owing to the prowess of Barnett, the Test match cricketer. He is a pleasant player to watch, both wicket-keeping and batting, and is a handsome, bronzed, blue-eyed man with a ready smile and a friendly manner.

Yesterday evening I sat on the grass with some others including Kevin Fegan, John Fairley of Divisional Headquarters, and a young MacAlister of the RAAF. Although only young, he has been outstanding in the things he has done. After we had listened to a gramaphone recital of the entire score of *The Pirates of Penzance* we all four went to Divisional Headquarters at the two-storied house over near the hospital gates. Here some played bridge, but I listened to MacAlister's story. He was shot down over Timor about 23 March, whilst he was on a reconnaissance flight from Darwin, just a month after the capitulation of the 40th Battalion (Colonel Leggatt) and the other troops in Timor. They all had to jump out over the forest and MacAlister's two fellow flyers, he thinks, were killed. His parachute opened and saved him. After varous adventures he was captured and put inside barbed wire with the prisoners from the 40th Battalion and coastal defence guns. He told some stories of one Armstrong, the freelance, and also of the independent force of Australians that is still supposed to be roaming the wilds of Timor.

Monday, 12 October

Classification Day. I inspected my 70-80 patients and discharged those who were fit to rejoin their units. At 5 p.m. I walked over to the AGH to attend one of Colonel Taylor's lectures — making sure to keep one eye on the gate as the last flag-ferry leaves at 6 p.m., often just ahead of time. The young Englishman in charge was kind enough to walk up to the hut where the lecture was taking place and advised me it was time to leave.

In the evening, Brian Ferguson of the 2/26th Battalion looked in to see me. He has been on a working party in Singapore for the last six months, where they lived in a comfortable house and had 'every modern convenience' and a great amount of latitude. For example, on one occasion he and a couple of other officers were allowed to go on a truck to Johore to buy pineapples for the 500-600 men in their party. They proceeded out into the country, ran out of petrol and were left there alone on parole, as it were, whilst the Japanese guard went back to get another truck which took some hours.

Wednesday, 14 October

Yesterday, Robin Orr and I had to return to the AGH for the morning. The occason was an inspection and enumeration of all hospital officers by the Japanese. It did not take long once the cars arrived and the Japanese officers alighted. We were lined up and counted — about 40 majors, 75 captains, a dozen lieutenants and one lonely second lieutenant.

About 1,500 Australians brought from Java last week were taken away today by steamers *Maebashi Maru* and *Tatsumo Maru* — smallish steamers of about 2,000 tons — for an unknown destination. Also, a large party went from here to Singapore as a working party, mostly 2/26th Battalion off again after a brief spell here. A party, led by John Oakeshott* of Lismore, left the hospital also, to look after the camp hospital.

Thursday, 15 October
A new system of Japanese pay came into force recently and today was our first pay day. The Japanese rate is $30 a month for officers. Of this amount, AIF Headquarters hold back half. What we actually received, therefore, and what we signed for, was $15. This represented pay for last month. AIF Headquarters subtract some for the hospital funds to buy extras for the hospital, and the rest goes to pay the men 10 cents a day to those not working. Working party members in town get paid by the Japanese 10 cents a day for privates and 15 cents for NCOs, but those not working or those in hospital don't receive anything.

Tonight had a pleasant game of bridge in my 'flat' — Jock White, MacAlister and Ferguson (of the Water and Sewerage Board, Sydney) made up for a foursome. For supper I gave them some compote of figs, made from dried figs I bought from the canteen and a cup of polimalt — a Chinese imitation, and a poor one, of Ovaltine.

Sunday, 18 October
I had an interesting trip this afternoon. I felt inquisitive about the American survivors of the U.S.A. cruiser *Houston*, and *Perth* survivors who are stationed at the southern area on the edge of the Straits, such a pretty place that a trip there is a pleasure under any circumstances. I was lucky in finding room on the daily ambulance which runs to the hospital at 3.30 p.m. After the hospital, it chanced that the ADMS wanted to go to the southern area so I had a ride all the way.

I found Americans and Australians all together in a long terrace of two stories facing the water under the big trees and in a garden of shrubs, frangipani, hibiscus and bougainvillea. I met Captain Kennedy of 2/3rd MG Battalion and Lieutenant Ransom and some other officers of that unit, and of the 2nd Pioneer Battalion, Lieutenant Mitchell, and also Commander Gunner Hawkins of *Perth*. Also Colonel Thorp of the 131st Field Artillery Regiment, U.S.A., and some of his officers and some survivors of *Houston* including a Jewish surgeon commander. Colonel Thorp has a beard, is a smart officer and a pleasant man. He told me that they had left the Philippines and had been diverted to Brisbane. However, after only four days there, early in December, they were sent on to Java. Hawkins of *Perth* told me something of the tragic last fight in the Sundar Straits. Captain Waller, he said, was last seen on the bridge by young Lieutenant Gay after the order to abandon ship had been given. He said to Gay, 'Clear out. Didn't you hear the order?' When Gay said, 'What about you, Sir?' Captain Waller had replied, 'I will be down presently'. Those whom I have met appear to have a great respect for Captain Waller.

*Dr John Oakeshott died in captivity.

Monday, 19 October

The Red Cross foodstuffs from South Africa, via India, have been most welcome. We have cocoa for breakfast and bully beef at least once a day in a good helping; also tinned vegetables, a welcome addition. Heartened as we are to receive these generous supplies, we wish sometimes they could send letters.

Thursday, 22 October

Visited the Lines of Communication area, round the corner and up the hill, about half a mile away. MacGregor of Toowoomba, for many months past, has run a poultry farm here and at present has two clutches of chickens out and a couple of dozen young ducks. One can buy the latter for 25 cents each at the canteen but they take three months to grow up. They seem to do well on rice and rice polishings plus chopped-up snails. The whole snail, in this part of the world, is about the same size as the duckling! By the way, for the last couple of months the Japanese, at our request, have sent us rice polishings as part of our diet — taste like bad pollard. The dose is two tablespoons a day, we boil it first and get it down somehow, generally mixed in food. MacGregor gave me six eggs for a lad in the Con-Depot who has optic neuritis. All eggs from here in the past months have gone to the hospital. He also gave me some chillies and long Chinese beans from a vegetable garden.

There don't appear to be any pests here, apart from mosquitoes; no hawks or butcher birds to prey upon the chickens.

In the evening, a major from the Gordon Highlanders, accompanied by a piper, gave us a talk on Regimental customs.

Friday, 23 October

In the evening I went on foot to the hospital — there was a meeting of the Changi Medical Society in the cinema, where papers were given by Charles Osborn and Major Doyle, RAMC.

As I was waiting at the gate to return with the 'flag ferry', I saw about 300 coloured or semi-coloured men in green uniforms from Java marching through the hospital area.

Saturday, 24 October

Living at the Convalescent Depot and eating with us now are Lieutenant Colonel Wright and other officers from L of C who had to vacate their house to make room for Dutchmen expected from Java.

This evening I attended a most interesting lecture in the Square by Lieutenant Hamelin of the U.S.A. cruiser *Houston*. He apologised for being dressed in khaki and for wearing a beard, the former dictated by force of circumstances and the latter being something to pull on occasionally!

Lieutenant Hamelin relived the tragic story of *Houston*'s last days, with touches of humour interspersed here and there. For well over an hour after twilight had faded and a full moon had risen behind a bank of cloud, he held a circle of 500 men enthralled as he recounted the Battle of Sourabaya.

On or about 20 February a mixed fleet of allied ships went out to meet the invading forces of Japan about 70 miles north. The fleet consisted of two Dutch cruisers *Deruyters* and *Java*, the famous British cruiser *Exeter*, HMAS *Perth*, and the U.S.A. cruiser *Houston*, as well as some Dutch and American destroyers. The enemy was too strong, however, especially the submarines, and the sea seethed with torpedoes. *Exeter* was crippled first and ordered out of the fight by the Dutch admiral. A few days later she was sunk after attempting to escape from Sourabaya. Later the two Dutch cruisers were sunk. *Houston* and *Perth* were compelled to break off the action and to make for Batavia under cover of darkness.

The following morning, orders were issued for *Houston* and *Perth* to get through the Sundar Straits between Java and Sumatra. But too late! That night they ran into a large Japanese landing force in the Straits and both ships were sunk after three-quarters of an hour's fight, during which *Houston*, although sinking, just kept on firing at a searchlight with her one remaining gun turret. Considerable damage was done to the enemy.

Lieutenant Hamelin, with two seamen, jumped from the forecastle into the sea, just a minute or two before *Houston* capsized and sank. They were in the water for an incredible number of hours, eventually landing on a small island, and some days later were taken to the mainland by launches sent from shore. By then, of course, everything was in the hands of the Japanese.

Monday, 26 October

We have heard that all, or most, of the British troops from southern area or from 18th Division are going, either overseas or to Thailand by train.

This evening the violinist Dennis East came to tea with our officers at the Convalescent Depot. Afterwards he gave an interesting talk to the convalescents on the story of the violin. Apparently Stradivarius lived to 90 years and made 2,000 violins. 'Of this number,' said Dennis, 'six hundred are reported to be in the U.S.A. The heyday of Stradivarius and his sons was the early eighteenth century, up to about 1730, and I think they sold their instruments for around ten pounds. The same now fetch up to £2,000 sterling. The violins had a special secret varnish and both wood and varnish dry and mellow with the years. This combination, together with their being original works of art, account for their high prices.

'After Stradivarius came another great Italian, Geranerius. Nowadays, in England, the leader is Arthur Hall of London with his small, select staff from the French school. He holds the secret of hand manufacture, of the moulding of the wood and the composition of the varnish. The latter is applied by coats, one coat every six months until 20 coats have been applied, i.e. ten years.'

After the talk, a few of us had supper of black tea and a couple of small, but real, biscuits upstairs with the two YMCA men, McNeilly and Ivor Hangar. Then the two latter had to take Dennis home to the 18th Division area as he had no flag. I decided to walk with them as far as our gate, and was glad to hear from East that the theatrical and concert group to which he belongs are not to be moved with the rest of the 18th Division. By some means or other, exemption for them had been obtained from the Japanese, so the Windmill Theatre will be able to carry on although it expects to be moved inside our wire.

Padre Haig, who runs the Windmill Choir, has lost half his singers. He had had a choir of about 40 and they had been practising the *Messiah* for Christmas — I had been fortunate on one occasion, prior to coming to this Depot, in being with East at a *Messiah* rehearsal and it was excellent.

Tuesday, 27 October

All the area of Selarang is very picturesque, apart from the Barrack Square. The officers of the Convalescent Depot have meals on the verandah of what used to be the Sergeants' Mess of the Gordon Highlanders. This, in common with all the buildings, has been spoiled by the splashing over of black paint which was hurriedly applied at the outbreak of war. There are also the usual scars on the walls from the flying splinters of air bombs.

The grass is waving high on all the slopes leading to the little gully below where the vegetable gardens are. Beyond the gardens, the long line of rusting barbed wire coils lie half hidden in the undergrowth that flanks the water course. On the slopes of the hill opposite, looking west from here, there are native huts, three or four of them, and cultivated pastures where some Chinese farmers and their women and children live. The huts are dark, untidy and thickly thatched. The farmers appear to live on their few vegetable patches and their clumps of banana trees, but their land lies outside the wire and represents freedom of a kind — the great world outside the prison area.

It is pleasant to hear faintly at times the shouts of children coming across the gully. At the very top of the hill is a shelter and a sentry box, and here we see every morning a Japanese 'changing of the guard' ceremony. There is a large light or lantern burning all night. A road passes the guardhouse along the crest of the hill, and natives passing on bicycles must alight and walk right up to the guard house and bow before remounting and proceeding on their lawful way. One can see their low bowings from our eating verandah.

As regards the Convalescent Depot's staff, there are only three medical officers — Colonel Webster, Captain Smith (from Wagga) and myself.

Wednesday, 28 October

Lieutenant Alan McLean, because of his amputated leg, is a permanent patient at the Convalescent Depot and it is very cheery to be with him. It is also good to have here Lindsay Orr, Andy Ferguson, Bill Dolamore and Bill Barnes, having known them all so long at the AGH. Probably Bob Seddon will soon be hobbling about over here and eventually young Reid who, poor fellow, still has the tube in his chest after all these months.

Today an exciting event took place. Alan McLean received a letter from a girl he had known in South Africa. This is the first postal message I have set eyes on since we were taken prisoner, and it gives promise of better things to come — the longed-for news from home. In the letter she said, 'we hope to get news through to you from Australia soon', so it would appear that shipping is the problem. I have long presumed that Britain and the U.S.A. are using all available shipping to reinforce Libya. It is my theory that a combined attack will be made there and a big decisive blow given to the Axis and, moreover, that this will be done soon before the winter.

We are still enjoying the last Red Cross supplies from South Africa. We have condensed milk for breakfast, one 12 oz tin serving 16 men per day makes a palatable dilution, and helps down the rice porridge. The Japanese have given up supplying us with wheat flour so we are bereft of our daily slice of bread (3 × 2 inches), but we have a dessertspoonful of sugar each per day (Red Cross) and take it at breakfast. For many weeks there was Red Cross cocoa for breakfast, made with water, and this was a respite from the eternal tea; however, the cocoa has now run out.

We still have a substantial slab of Red Cross bully beef every day or two and the Japanese give us fresh frozen mutton about once a week. Then there is the supply of Red Cross 'dahl' — little split peas or lentils from India — so we don't do so badly. Alan McLean's letter was from a Mrs Lacy of Durban — formerly a nurse in Dr Postes' rooms in Macquarie Street; it was dated Durban, 15 July.

The YMCA men, McNeilly and Hangar, are doing a good job here. They are both musical, especially McNeilly, and something is arranged each night to entertain the patients. Tonight McNeilly asked me and some others to his room and we had a good hour of gramophone records, including some good ones of *Madam Butterfly*.

Thursday, 29 October

Lieutenant Colonel Leggatt, who is attached here, had to go with Carrick and others from Timor to be interviewed today by the Japanese. They were questioned about Darwin — no coercion was used. This afternoon Lieutenant Colonel Glyn White, ADMS held a conference at Convalescent Depot for the medical officers of this area. Whilst we were meeting upstairs, we saw through the windows the arrival of a lorry-load of Dutch troops from Java. We have been expecting them for days. Various shades of colour, from pure Dutch to almost pure native, and various uniforms, chiefly their Robin Hood green shorts and jackets. The officers wore high peaked caps and big badges, at first sight like the Germans'.

MacAlister is in charge of a squad of men who are carpenters, and they proceed every day to the big Changi Gaol a couple of miles up the road to erect fittings and sleeping bunks into the buildings. Mac told me that Lady Heath is still very ill in the Gaol Hospital over there. She has been ill since her baby was stillborn many months ago. It is sad for the General.

These nights it rains almost regularly and often my bed and I have to be moved in a hurry from the balcony where I sleep, into the hot and mosquito-ridden room. If a strong wind comes with the rain squall, as it so often does, the men on the windward side of this floor get flooded out, for all doors have long since been removed for the sake of the timber.

N.B. More on Alan McLean's letter — it was marked in English and Dutch (opened by the censor). There was no Japanese mark at all, but it arrived slit open at one end, and the address was simply 'AIF, Malaya'.

Sunday, 1 November
In the afternoon, I walked half a mile along the bitumen road, down the hill and then up the hill to General Sir Lewis Heath's house.* I wanted to enquire after his wife and to ask if he knew General de Wiart and Dr Wallace of Singapore (Tan Toch Sang Hospital) and to find out if the latter was in Changi Gaol. I did not think he would mind an unofficial call from an unknown captain seeing we were all POWs together. The General lives in a red-tiled bungalow with a couple of his staff captains and a few batmen. The place was deserted, everything wide open including an out-of-use WC. I went around to the back door and was met by a batman who took me to the General. I sat in an antiquated arm chair while he sat at his desk. In the background was a photo of Lady Heath. He told me she had aplastic anaemia and that Wallace, who was looking after her at Changi Goal Hospital, held out no hope unless she could be got out of the country. The poor woman has had 13 blood transfusions. He said Dr Wallace was well. A Japanese doctor came over to tell him how his wife was a few days previously and he much appreciated this; however, it is three weeks since he has been permitted to see her.

I only stayed ten minutes, as he had an appointment, but he was most pleasant and courteous.

Tuesday, 3 November
In the evening there was a lecture on Thailand, delivered in the Square by Major Laming, ex-judge of Thailand. He described conditions of the country, climate, food, scenery, etc., and this was interesting as many British troops are on their way there to a camp near Bangkok.

Wednesday, 4 November
In the evening there was a lecture on Thailand, delivered in the Square by Major Laming, ex-judge of Thailand. He described conditions of the

*GOC, 3rd Indian Corps.

country, climate, food, scenery, etc., and this was interesting as many British troops are on their way there to a camp near Bangkok.

Wednesday, 4 November
In the early morning all the British troops of the 3rd Indian Corps, who have been in the Square in barracks opposite to us, paraded for departure, about 400 men and 200 officers. After a long wait about 10 lorries arrived to take them all off to the railway to entrain for Thailand. All seemed well and in good spirits, many looking quaint in the new civilian-type felt hats which have arrived, together with boots, as part of Red Cross supplies. General Sir Lewis Heath was there to wave them goodbye. I felt sad to see them go; only a few are left here now. Each truck was driven by an Indian, presumably working for the Japanese either voluntarily or compulsorily.

Tonight there was a 'blackout' — Japanese order — so we all had to do without any lights after dark.

Thursday, 5 November — another blackout tonight.

Sunday, 8 November
Armistice Day is to be remembered this year. Last year, when I was with the 22nd Brigade at Mersing, the day went unobserved, which seemed to me a pity. So today there was a voluntary parade on the Square at 4 p.m. About 300-400 AIF men paraded and the bearers of the wreaths fell in on the right. The wreaths were a surprise because there must have been much preparation in these last few days but there was no outward sign of this. Many were of large proportions and all were well made. Some were quite works of art — interlaced patterns of flowers and leaves, frangipani, bougainvillea, hibiscus, cassia and *Bignonia venusta*. Lieutenant Colonel Webster led our party from the Convalescent Depot and we marched off to the beat of a side-drummer and tune of a Gordon Highlander piper who led the way, down the mile that leads to the AIF cemetery. The assembled troops inside the cemetery took the form of a hollow square.

The C of E Chaplain in Chief, Padre Jones, led the prayers, and a piano accordian gave the lead for the hymns. Padre Benjamin of AGH also took part, and an officer sang a solo, a piece I had not heard before. It was a solemn yet stirring occasion. All felt it had been a worthy commemoration.

On the march back, as we swung back into the gate through the barbed wire, there on the right of the road stood General Heath and, with him, Colonel Galleghan. As the order 'eyes right' rang out, all heads were held high and the arms swung a little more briskly. I think every man in the AIF here has a high regard for the one-armed General and all have had an opportunity of getting to know him since his lectures on the Malayan Campaign and on the victorious Eritrean Campaign when his Indian Division took Kerren and Kassawa.

This area is now well-populated with Dutchmen of all shades of colour! The men salute smartly and the officers are courteous and pleasant. Many are of very fine physique and many are elderly grey-headed men, evidently the home-guard of Java. It is rather comical to see some of them swinging and bending at the physical training parade held each morning in the Square before breakfast. They are attached to the AIF for rations and discipline.

Padre McNeil held the usual Church Service in the evening on the area in front of the Convalescent Depot building: a lovely spot in the evenings with the sunset away to the left, and the waters of the Straits shimmering amongst the green hills and islands to the north. He dwelt on the theme of Armistice Day. If only men would go to Church, that is young men, in peacetime, and would sing hymns as they sing them here, the Church would be a force in the land. Admittedly here it is compulsory attendance, but there is nothing compulsory about the way the men sing, the splendid ring of their voices is most inspiring.'

Monday, 9 November
Among the blessings sent to the prisoners of war here are numerous pairs of black leather boots. They have not arrived too soon as it was only a matter of time before the majority of the troops would have been walking barefoot.

Wednesday, 11 November
At 11 a.m. bugles sounded. I was standing on my balcony thinking of Tony Rowan, Harold Woodford, Bill McCowan, Lee Pulling and a score of others who have given their lives in this war and the last. I was facing the Barrack Square and it was most moving to see how all stopped in their tracks at the sound of the bugle and stood to attention for the two minutes. A hush fell over the whole area.

In the evening, Ivor Hangar and I went across to 18th Division hoping to see the show at the Windmill Theatre. Reaching the theatre we found that the whole show had now broken up owing to all the troop movements lately. Too sad!

Friday, 13 November
Tonight and tomorrow night are blackouts, by order of the Japanese, so no one looks forward to two evenings of gloom.

Just before dark this evening, Jock White and MacAlister came up to my room bearing a large tin of asparagus. We opened it and demolished its contents, yarning in the darkness about old days.

The mosquitoes have not been too bad these last few days. Some nights they have been most troublesome, although not as noisy as their Australian relations. Unfortunately, the anopheles is around again as one of my patients developed a sudden high fever yesterday — a man who had had no previous malaria. Sergeant Matthews next door, in the 2nd Mobile Pathology Lab, found subtertian malaria in his blood film, a heavy infection, so I sent him off in the ambulance to AGH today.

Two new problems have arisen:

1. We now have an increased native reservoir here with the arrival of all the coloured Dutch from Java, and

2. There is a great shortage of mosquite nets — some having worn out and others having walked away.

Lieutenant Hamelin, U.S. Navy, came to the evening meal. The QM, Fred Anderson, excelled himself tonight with tomato soup, bully beef pie and apple tart! The latter was made from dried apples bought at the canteen and quite a good pastry had been made from maize flour.

The Red Cross supply from South Africa, the last and second addition, has improved our food rations to the extent that we have the occasional meat and vegetables out of tins and bully beef about once a week. The latter is in addition to the Japanese fresh meat supply, which is sent to us twice a week. This fresh supply is supposed to be 6 oz per man, but by the time one receives it it is about 2 oz, one small slice each. A certain amount of maize flour helps to make pastry of a sort and there was also a small quantity of tinned fruit.

The tide of war will again be surging over Tony's resting place in Tobruk.* If it is to be a victorious advance on our part, it is sad to think that he is not to share the thrill and reap some reward for the months of brave defensive struggle in which he took part early last year and up to when he fell in July.

Friday, 20 November

It is now not allowed to go between prison areas unless one has a pass and is on official duty. I obtained a pass today, and in the afternoon attended a meeting of the Changi Medical Society at the hospital. Bruce Hunt and Captain Cruickshank read papers on encephalitis. I took the opportunity of calling at the Officers' Ward to see Jock White who has just been admitted with some digestive trouble and, also, to have a small operation. He seemed cheery and promised me to stop smoking.

I also went to see some other friends and acquaintances amongst the patients, Ken Turich and Jack Marsden, Sid Bignell (Coomera) and Jock Douglas. Amongst the staff I saw Geoff Davies, Padre Pain and Bernard Clarke. The latter told me he had received a letter from Mrs Preston, wife of the U.S.A. Consul at Lourenço Marques. The Prestons used to live in Brisbane. The letter, written on 10 September, arrived a few days ago from Africa. She said that Mrs Clarke and family had gone to Melbourne. It was a comfort to hear that a link had been established, a one-way link it is true, but it makes me sick with anxiety and disappointment to know that, even at that late date, they had had no news about us here. What is wrong? One took it for granted that, months ago, word would have got through to say who was here; those from Java said that they understood that, whilst prisoners there, their names had been sent by wireless to Australia. No doubt they were correct. Mrs

*Charles Huxtable's brother-in-law, Tony Rowan.

Preston just said that there had been no news about those in Singapore.

Monday, 23 November
Padre Pain came over from the hospital and had lunch with me. He is a nice, kindly man — this Church man from Ballarat. I was sorry to hear that he expects to be sent from the hospital to a working party in Singapore. He mentioned that the mural drawings (the life-size Christmas scene) had been completed by the young Englishman over at his Chapel at the hospital. I must remember to have a look at it next time I'm over there.

I forgot to say that there was an address by Captain Kennedy of 2/3rd MG Battalion on Saturday afternoon to assembled officers about the war in Syria, July 1941. Very interesting. Kennedy is a Tasmanian and looks a good soldier. He worked in Syria with British troops and said they were second to none and he had been proud to be attached to them.

Today there was another lecture by young Captain Bishop who was part of the Blackforce (Brigadier Blackburn) defending Western Java. The latter fell in March and this particular force fought west of Bandoeng and fell back on this place.

Friday, 27 November
For the past week there has been no cocoa so we have black tea again at breakfast.

There is great interest everywhere now in the fighting in Libya and in North Africa. We read about it in the *Syonan Times*, copies of which come out here every few days.

I saw a few days ago that General Beckwith-Smith, the Commander of the 18th Division here in Malaya, had died of diphtheria at a POW camp somewhere unnamed, we think Formosa. Our senior officers, including Colonel Pigdon, will be there, wherever it is. One hopes that there is no epidemic of diphtheria but I don't like the sound of it. The newspaper article states that the late general was a friend of Lord Gowrie, Governor General of Australia.

Yesterday evening a Japanese Corporal, followed by a private soldier with a rifle, went through this area and accosted several men for not saluting. One of our patients was sitting on his bed and did not stand up because he did not see the Japanese soldiers passing by. He was called out on the road and spoken to severely.

Captain Alan Carrick agreed to come with me to General Sir Lewis Heath's house to say good-bye to him. We had just heard that he is being taken away tomorrow. (Brigadier Maxwell of the AIF 27th Brigade is to go also.) We arrived at the back door because the front door was once again deserted. We found that the General had just started his evening meal so we left a message and were turning away but were overheard and were requested to step inside. Sir Lewis Heath stood up and chatted with us for several minutes. He had seen his wife today to say goodbye.

She, of course, is still in hospital. We wished him good luck, saluted, shook hands and departed. Some would say it was a presumptuous visit but neither Alan Carrick nor I could see it in that light. We both wanted to say goodbye to a man who has been, in many ways, a guiding light to all here, a personality who has been respected and loved by the AIF as well as the British troops.

I had arranged with MacAlister and Cribb (of Ipswich) to visit the AIF concert party show and met them at the theatre door at 8 p.m. Before the show I had a talk with the principal commedienne, Jack Smith, formerly the tap-dancer of Southport who once taught my twins some lessons in the art. I remember Barby and Libby chattering and laughing about the antics of Jack Smith before I ever met him.

Saturday, 28 November
Early breakfast and then hurried across before 9.30 a.m. to No. 3 gate to the farewell muster. AIF troops and the few remaining Tommies lined the bitumen from the General's drive to No. 3 gate. He walked through and, as I approached, I could hear the successive cheers from the different units and the AIF Orchestral Band playing bravely at the gate. At the gate, it was quite informal. Little groups of people, mostly officers, stood about and chatted and the General moved amongst them making adieus. I saw many people I knew and shook hands with Brigadier Maxwell; he looked well, not so thin. He and his brother, Major Maxwell, who stays behind, stood side by side, a fine-looking pair of men, each well over 6 feet tall. Everybody laughed and tried to be gay, but it was hard when the band played 'Auld Lang Syne' to keep back a slight moisture of the eye.

A motor lorry, not even a car, came to take the General away! It stopped 100 yards away on the main road and a solitary Japanese officer walked up. The Sikh guards at the guardhouse hard by roared themselves into a frenzied position of salute as the Japanese officer passed them. The latter indicated quite amicably to General Heath that it was time to go, at the same time looking a little nonplussed, I thought, at the sight of the send-off and the sound of the music. As the party passed through the gate, Brigadier Maxwell's faithful little batman (also an ex-soldier of the last war), with some others, brought up the rear with the scanty luggage on a small trailer. In the distance we watched them getting into the back of the motor truck and move off. And so it all ended, a pleasant little ceremony albeit a sad one.

During the morning, also, I visited the vegetable garden down the depression on the western side of our area. No vegetables at present but my object was to find derris plant growing. The orderly Murphy and I and another man, one of the gardeners, found and dug some up. The roots go very deep and the original planters of them had very cunningly planted each with the root tied with a single knot. By loosening the sandy soil and then putting a hand through the loop, it was possible to haul up a few feet of root to each small plant. Murphy and I crushed some roots and soaked them in a petrol tin — I want to try them for bed bugs! All the buildings have now a liberal population of *Cinax lectuarius* and the men have to work hard to keep their beds clear enough of the pests to get any sleep for themselves. I have tried derris solution — made by pounding and then soaking the roots in water — on the bugs and it appears to kill them in a minute or two if one puts plenty on (no use spraying it on).

In the evening Major Robertson of the 2/2nd Gurkha Regiment came up to see me. He was in the 29th Division in France in the last war. Sergeant Major Rogerson, formerly of 1st Lancashire Fusiliers, now a member of the AIF, is a patient of mine here and I asked him up too because Major Robertson's regiment of those days — the 1st Royal Fusiliers — was brigaded with the 1st Lancashire Fusiliers. So the three of us had a great talk about old scenes and people of the last war. We yarned for two hours, during which time I made some coffee (with a teaspoon of sugar in each cup) and the Major had a supply of Chinese cigars.

Sunday, 29 November
Mother's birthday, bless her; if there were only some news from those at home! I have recently read the clauses of the International Agreement about conditions and care of prisoners of war. It states that letters shall be limited to not more than one a week, each to consist of not more than one page written on both sides. It is now ten months since any of us have received anything by post with the exception of the lucky three who have had a letter from people in South Africa.

Monday, 21 December
A week ago yesterday I had to leave my quarters on the first floor of this building and move to Alan Carrick's room on the top floor, south-east corner of balcony. Quite roomy enough for the two of us and a lovely extensive view of the east and north. My former corner is taken over as headquarters of the Dutch soldiery in the Barrack Square.

Today, Carrick and I have just had orders that we are to move back to where I was a week ago. Meantime, one floor of this building, the top floor, goes to the 9th Field Ambulance. Major Burnside and all my 80 convalescent patients are concentrated on the ground floor instead of on two floors. They seem quite happy, crowded together on their rickety iron beds on their filthy mattresses without sheets, the lucky man with a blanket or pillow, and plenty of bugs, of course. One means of reducing the infestation is to put beds on an ant heap. The ants attack the bugs.

I shall be sorry to leave this top floor. There is nearly always a pleasant breeze, which makes the nights cool enough for a blanket and a coat so that one can sleep comfortably, to be roused in the morning by the bugles sounding Reveille and the sergeant major on the floor below banging on the iron ring which he keeps suspended by a rope for use as a kind of ship's bell or fire tocsin.

It is encouraging to watch the sunrise. The dawn always brings hope and helps to dispel loneliness and lethargy. The novelty of this life has long worn off and the prolonged rest and inactivity and monotony weigh like a load on mind and spirit. I do not mean that hope goes, for I think it would be true to say that every man here is optimistic; that is to say that he feels and believes that we shall all be home some day. However, there are times when the futility of this waiting and all the petty activities associated with our daily life here becomes the dominant note which renders discordant, not only the never-ending bugle calls, but also conversation, rumours, news and jokes, which clangs its melancholy even into the thought of tomorrows. I suppose at my stage of life one must expect something of this. The young are too full of animal spirits and of endless years ahead of them to worry about the wastage of a few months or even, for that matter, a few years.

Whether it be the life or the diet, or both, I find difficulty in reading. (The specialists do give it a name, which is really a laziness of the accommodating muscles of the eyes, just as all one's muscles become lazy and lethargic here.) I have to wear my two pairs of glasses together to read comfortably at normal range whereas 12 months ago I could thread a needle without either and certainly never required a pair of glasses to read a newspaper. Also, there is the difficulty of memorising — here I am again, three weeks gone, another gap to fill in my diary.

Why are all the troops returning from Singapore? Has there been an attack on Burma? One rumour is that the natives are complaining to the Japanese of all the unemployment occasioned by the work done by prisoners of war. I think this is merely rumour.

December has brought with it the pleasant north-east breeze, making this the coolest and most pleasant time of the year.

Christmas preparations, 1942
Throughout December, in little scattered groups, the men have been making Christmas presents for the children in Changi Gaol. A week before Christmas these were sent across (for which permission was sought and granted by the Japanese) to our entertainment hall at the main building of the Convalescent Building to be on display. The collection would not have disgraced the toy department of David Jones or Farmers, the ingenuity, the patience and the kindly thoughts behind it all combined to make one feel the kind of happiness that is near to the shedding of a tear. No doubt many were thinking of their own little ones at home as they made their gifts for the little strangers inside the big walls along the road.

The Gaol is only half a mile away but until Christmas Day nobody from here ever saw inside the high wall which surrounds the acre of ground which is the world of these women and children over there. On Christmas Day about two dozen Army people who had relatives there were allowed to visit the Gaol. Only one Australian, I believe, could lay claim to such a visit. Captain Ennis of the BGH told me that he was allowed exactly half an hour with his wife. He said that they all looked well and happy and quite well dressed. Every couple of weeks they are allowed to visit the beach for half an hour or so under guard.

During the days before Christmas Day, the AIF working parties began to arrive back in their thousands from Singapore. The great Barrack Square and its surrounding three-storied buildings began to fill to overflow. The last detachment arrived on the 29th, a torrent of rain drenched the Square and the men and their baggage as they were unloading the trucks. The latter were loaded to perilous heights with extraordinary collections of what appeared to be mere junk. Ancient and blackened boilers and cooking utensils, improvised beds, tables and other 'furniture', stacks of weatherbeaten kit bags, loads of tins and boxes, mostly empty and battered. The whole 12,000 of us must be back again.

The British troops, of course, went to Southern Area and 18th Division area and 11th Division area, the latter just opposite us on the other side of the Singapore-Changi Road. Thus, in November the Barrack Square had been emptied of all remaining troops north to Bangkok in order to make room for six to eight hundred Dutch. Then the latter, in turn, were emptied out and sent to Southern Area two miles away to make room for the return of the AIF to this Square. The Square has become a crowded thoroughfare and the buildings a clamour of noisy voices and boots on concrete stairways, silent only during mealtimes and after lights out.

December has seen the finish of all meat rations and the Japanese have announced that there is no more meat to be issued. Occasionally, we are to have fish. On one occasion there were prawns which not one of us could eat as they looked and tasted too stale. Another time I had a steak, size about 3 × 2 inches, of stingray and it was quite nice. Apart from these rare ocasions, we are now vegetarian because tinned fish can no longer be bought at the canteen; we hope it will again become procurable as it is a great help even at the price of a dollar for a tin of herrings. We make one tin do for four. The condensed milk, which came from the South African Red Cross and which provided us for many weeks with a helpful liquid on our rice porridge at breakfast, has now quite cut out as a general issue. There is still some in the Red Cross store at the hospital, but it is now used only for patients and those cases of malnutrition at the Convalescent Depot which we recommend for supplementary diets. The brown rice porridge is much improved, I find, by mixing a few peanuts with it and then sprinkling on the one level dessertspoon of sugar which is our daily ration from the Japanese. If this sugar is kept back by the Quartermaster for another dish such as a pudding at night, one has to go without for breakfast. But I must say I enjoy my morning porridge and the black tea helps to wash it down. I seldom if ever get headaches on this fat-free diet with a minimum of sugar.

Christmas Day

Christmas Day was a really happy day for all as I went early with my friend, Frank Wright of the Red Cross, who has now come to the Convalescent Depot, to the bamboo chapel near the AIF Headquarters, known as St Andrews. Here Padre Jones, senior AIF Chaplain, administered Holy Communion. We saw Sergeants Downer and Newson there, and walked back with them. A holiday air reigned and much sound of carols and Christmas hymns. On Christmas Eve the Convalescent Depot choir, under George McNeilly and Ivor Hangar, did the rounds of the Barrack Square with a small portable hand organ and gave the great buildings in turn a few of the old sweet tunes. 'Holy Night,' is very popular here.

On Christmas afternoon, various units held entertainments and games. By now, a large part of the AIF working troop had returned from Singapore city and the various work camps scattered about the island; the last few hundred did not arrive until about 28 December. Nevertheless, on Christmas afternoon there was a vast crowd of men who came to see the fun at our particular sports ground, which is the cricket ground in front of the big, main building of the Convalescent depot. This grassy area is semi-circular, sloping sharply around its circumference to a valley below where vegetables are grown. Pleasant shade trees, and flowering shrubs fringe the margin. The buildings and the ground face northward to the distant waters of the Straits of Johore a mile away, while on clear days dim blue mountains can be seen 30 miles away, one of which I am sure, from its contour and flattened top, is the mountain called Panti at Kota Tinggi.

To return to Christmas festivities, 1942, there was a good program of sports including relay races, tugs of war, wood chops, throwing cricket balls, etc., also some stalls and sideshows provided coconut shies, etc. And so passed Christmas Day very happily. That evening at the theatre building, there was a crowded attendance at a sacred concert to which Carrick and Frank Wright and I went together.

December-January 1942-3

As regards other events during December, which it may be of interest to record, were the following:

The Japanese instituted a system of parades at which, about 7 p.m., each formation must be on parade for the purpose of being counted. When we are all on parade on the Barrack Square, or at the various other parade grounds scattered about the area, a motor truck drives into the area and drops a Japanese NCO and a couple of private soldiers at each point. We are called to attention and have to salute the NCO which he returns ceremoniously in Japanese fashion, holding hand at the salute and bowing at the same time in all directions. We then number off and are counted by the Japanese soldiers, then more saluting and off they go and we are dismissed. In the early mornings we hold our own system of role call parades without the visits of the Japanese.

During December and up to 11 January, a course of lectures in malaria was held at the British Hospital on Mondays and Thursdays. Lieutenant Colonel Strachan was the leading teacher — soft Irish voice, tremendous enthusiast — he comes from the Government Institute at Kuala Lumpur where he worked with the world-famous Dr Field, Chief Malariologist of the FMS Medical Services. I attended the course walking across twice a week. It ended with a walk of inspection for several miles outside the wire, i.e. outside the prison area. We medical officers had special permission to make this tour with Lieutenant Colonel Strachan and were not in any way put on parole, except in so far as we have all signed the famous pledge. Good work has been done by Strachan and others all round this area. Before the war the area was practically free of malaria and of anopheles, but a couple of months neglect following the confusion after the surrender, aggravated by the fact that bomb bursts had destroyed drains, soon produced breeding of anopheles mosquitoes resulting in an outbreak of malaria amongst our troops in the prison area. The Japanese then authorised us to carry out what preventive measures we could, and anti-malarial work was instituted under the direction of Strachan with good effect, although he had insufficient oil and gear and labour to work with. Recently the Japanese have taken it on themselves, and we now see occasional Tamils going around with sprays or working on drains. Lieutenant Colonel Strachan said he nearly cried with homesickness when he saw the Tamils. He says the Indians are out on their own as regards anti-malarial labour.

On a Sunday in mid-December (13th), the medical officers of this area played a cricket match against the Australian MOs from the hospital. Bert Nairn captained the latter team, Colonel Webster captained ours. We played on the padang across the road from here in the 11th Division area. It reminded me of that October Sunday afternoon in 1941 when I saw the Gordons play the Argyles on that same ground.

Another entertainment in mid-December was the AIF concert party which, at its large centre, put on a very good pantomime, *Cinderella*. Jack Smith of Southport provided a comical turn as one of the two ugly sisters; the other was equally ugly and almost as funny.

During this period one had opportunities to get outside the wire on trailer parties. Our unit sends two kinds of trailer parties, one to collect salt water, the other to collect wood.

The salt water parties go about a mile or more under coconut groves, over sandy stretches and through avenues of scrub and lantana to a sandy beach on the southern coast. If the tide is well in, it is possible to strip off and have a swim in the sea, a grand experience which I enjoyed on one occasion with Jock White and another time with Leslie Greener. At such times, the filling of the empty drums on the trailers is carried out by a few conscientious workers whilst the rest disport themselves and lash the limpid, lapping wavelets into a foam of ecstasy. The two or three Japanese guards who are on duty at this beach regard us indifferently. On one occasion I saw about 30 or 40 Australians heading for the open sea with masterful crawl strokes, and I wondered how far they would be allowed to go before the guards took a shot at them. Later, unfortunately, a Japanese order prohibited bathing.

The wood parties go along the main road outside the wire towards the big Gaol, then turn left past the huge area that is now the big vegetable area worked by the Japanese with prisoners of war. After half a mile or more through vegetable gardens, the wood trailers plunge into a rubber tree plantation and here the forestry squads, British and Australian, are hard at work cutting down rubber wood for fuel. It seems to be a dispensation of Providence on our behalf that rubber wood can be burnt as fuel as soon as cut. It is the only wood I know which can be used like this.

In the early days of captivity, an AIF Education Centre was formed by several people including, I think, Brigadier Taylor and Adrian Curlewis. It later came under the direction of Captain Leslie Greener of Sydney, who was aided by Sergeants Alec Downer of Adelaide, David Griffin of Leura, Kelynack of Sydney, Newsome and Private Blakey. They make a good team and are a nice lot of fellows. David Griffin gave an excellent course of lectures on English literature, one night a week for about a month. I used to meet Jim Crombie there regularly. Alec Downer also gave a course of lectures on civics. He is a barrister from England, as well as Australia, and an Oxford graduate, a very cultured and agreeable personality.

The Education Centre is kept supplied with a copy of occasional editions of *Syonan* (Singapore) *Times* which is still published in English and provides us with a certain amount of outside news. The circulating library is not very big and, as it is used by the whole AIF area, it is hard to get books out which one wants. Lectures and addresses are given in the big hall at the Convalescent Depot main building, and the hall is usually packed to capacity because such lectures, etc., are open to all from the prison area.

A patient at the Convalescent Depot lent me a leather-bound volume of Macaulay which he had retrieved somewhere or other and I gained a great deal of enjoyment and of instruction out of reading his revues of historical matters. I also much enjoyed the thrilling story of Dunkirk by John Masefield, *The Nine Days Wonder*.

New Year's Eve

The Japanese Army supplied us with some liquor, about 1 oz. per man. It tasted like a mixture of brandy and dry sherry. It was not saki. Alan Carrick and I did not drink our ration at the evening meal, but kept it to bring up to our room for New Year celebrations. Hither also came Dave Hinder, MO of the 2/18th and 2/19th Battalions, Dick Pockley of the 2/20th Battalion, and Frank Wright of the Red Cross who now lives at this Convalescent Depot. Our batman Eldridge (the sailor) had the table set out on our little bit of balcony under the electric light, table cloth, flowers and all! We lucky ones in this building are the only people in the whole Barrack Square area who have the electric light laid on. It is a concession to the fact that this is a medical building with patients, although the 80 patients are entirely accommodated on the ground floor.

We five yarned and joked until, shortly before midnight, a Highland piper appeared in the semi-darkness of the Barrack Square below and, surrounded by a crowd of cheering Australians, he serenaded each building in turn. At midnight there was a beating of gongs and tins in the time-honoured fashion and we five sang 'Auld Lang Syne'. Dick Pockley gave us a toast — 'absent friends' — and each of us became a little absent-minded after that, no doubt. Then we toasted the fighting men of our own forces and those of our allies who are still carrying on the fight overseas and in different lands.

1943

5-10 January

The Changi Conference of Constructive Christianity (CCCC) organised by Padre Jones, Senior Chaplain, and Padre McNeil of this Depot, lasted six successive nights and each night there was a different speaker. Each address was followed by questions from the audience. Many questions were political rather than sociological or spiritual, but there was no doubt about the great interest shown or about the evidence of that hidden interest in religion which can be aroused in almost every man.

The speakers were Padre Barrett, Ivor Hangar (YMCA), Captain Woodruff, Padre Foster-Haig a visitor from the 18th English Division, Padre Polaine of the 2/26th Battalion. The last night there was no address, just questions only. The Conference was closed with prayer by Padre Jones on the last night, Sunday. He announced, too, that the Conference would be followed by a series of different classes held weekly to study different subjects allied to the matters discussed at the main conference. I decided to attend Alec Downer's class on Government and possibly also Woodruff's class on International Affairs. It provides interest and I think does good for people to interchange ideas and to learn how to do this without rancour.

Thursday, 11 January

Returning from the hospital I saw numbers of laden motor trucks bearing men along the distant Changi Road into 18th Division area. I heard later that this was a big arrival from Java — 1,500 AIF and 500 Dutch. Of the AIF total, about 500 went to 11th Division area.

Friday June 26th 1942

PROGRAMME.

1. **Reginald Renison** - - - **Pianoforte.**

   4 Preludes   )
   Nocturne   )   Chopin
   Valse   )
   Fantasia - Impromptu)

2. **Georse Wall** - - - - - **Baritone.**

   The Question .. ..Schubert
   Droop not young lover .. .. Handel
   To the Forest .. .. Tschaikowsky.
   The Lute Player .. .. ..Watson

3. **Denis East** - - - - - - **Violin.**

   Preludium & Allegro   Kreisler
                              "Paganini"
   Air on the G String .. .. .. Bach
   Introduction & Rondo Capriccioso
                          C.Saint Saens

4. **John Foster** - - - - - **Tenor.**

   My Dreams .. .. Tosti
   Who is Sylvia .. .. .. Schubert
   I know of two bright eyes ..Clutsam
   Lend me your aid .. .. .. Gounod

ooOoo

GOD SAVE THE KING.

ooOoo

Programme for a concert held on 26 June 1942

Australian prisoners at Changi moving to Selarang Barracks Square, September 1942

A contemporary drawing of Australian and other prisoners of war herded into Selarang Square, September 1942. They stayed there until signing their undertaking not to attempt to escape

Contemporary cartoon by George Sprod

Japanese money, often known as 'Occupation Money', issued to captives

Smoke-oh was a prisoner-of-war journal painted by the cartoonist George Sprod and circulated to the sick bays

On Sunday evening Griffith brought to tea at our table Lieutenant Uroe of the 2/26th Battalion. This officer served for a time with Shanghai volunteers and is very interesting. That was a volunteer force in the old days before he went to Australia which protected the international settlement in Shanghai. He met Dr O'Hara there and several others whom Barbara and I met when we were up there in 1935.

Thursday, 18 January
Captain Laurie West of the Gurkhas came to see Alan Carrick today with interesting news. He has been to the Gaol today under orders to attend the Japanese authorities there and he was handed a wireless message from Delhi, India, from his wife. It was to the effect that, last May, his wife had given birth to twin boys and all were well. He was allowed to send a message in reply. Old Laurie, of course, is filled with delight and pride. We later gave him a special evening up here and, in the presence of a dozen of his friends, drank his health in black coffee and shared a fairly good feed of fried rice cakes and fruit salad made of pineapple and paw paw.

I had about this time a surprise visit from V.T. McGuire of Southport. How strange that we should have met here. His wife used to show me photographs of him on active service in Palestine and Egypt way back in 1940 before I ever had any prospects of serving abroad. He looks well, though thin and weatherbeaten. Whilst in the Middle East, he was taken from his Battalion and attached to Headquarters of the 7th Division. He left Suez early in February for Australia on *Orcades* but, unfortunately, they were sidetracked and landed first at Sumatra and then at Java shortly before the surrender, and that is how he came to be here. He came twice to see me, a longish walk from the 18th Division area, but I was able to help him with some socks, etc., and a little money. He left again with the Java party on 21 January for up-country; we think probably near Bangkok but nobody knows for certain.

Friday, 26 January
Australia Day was remembered and celebrated by a parade in the Square. The drill was excellent and the sight impressive, albeit, unarmed. Colonel Galleghan took the salute of the march past. There was even a Union Jack flying and two pipers with a detachment of Australian drummers, side and tenor drums.

Sunday, 28 January
Met Russell Braddon, grandson of Sir Harry Braddon of Sydney, and Peter Minnett, son of Dr Roy Minnett of Manly, old boys of North Shore and both gunners in the 2/15th Regiment. A nice pair. Young Minnett knew Duncan McKie — he was in camp at Cowra, N.S.W.

Wednesday, 3 March
I had the evening meal with Carl Furner at the hospital, the first meal

in the old Mess since I left them last October. Afterwards, we walked up to the British officers place and heard the story of a ship which was sunk last 2 January off the west coast of Africa by a German raider. The lecturer was the Captain. He and 24 others were the sole survivors of 58 men. The Germans just opened fire without warning and destroyed the ship in a few minutes with their heavy guns; later, a boat lowered by the Germans raced round them and raked their decks with machine guns, smashing every lifeboat and raft. They were given no chance to surrender and the survivors leapt into the sea. The Germans picked up 28 men, some of whom died; the remainder were treated very well, a favourite German method of placating the survivors of an outrage. They were eventually landed at Batavia and handed over to the Japanese.

Friday, 5 March
Mrs Doris Booth's country (New Guinea) must be a centre of activity these days. I remember her favourite hymn, 'Oh happy band of pilgrims'.

Today we heard the wonderful news that there are bags of mail for us!! After all these months! They are at Changi Gaol and we must patiently wait, perhaps for days or weeks until they are sorted, or perhaps months if they have to be censored first.

There was a lecture today by Colonel Bye at the hospital, very well delivered and most interesting.

To go back to 15 February, the miserable anniversary of the loss of Malaya by the British, 120 years after the death of Raffles, founder of Singapore. It is to be hoped that the spirit of the great man does not know, or if he does know, that, at least, his knowledge may be assuaged by foresight of things to come. For the Japanese Army it was naturally a great anniversary and the *Syonan Times* advertised various sporting events in honour of the occasion, even a marathon relay race down the peninsular from Penang. Opposite our quarters, here beyond the gully and the wire, one can see a peasant hut with a Japanese flag hung out for the occasion. On three mornings all troops except sick or disabled were marched to the large playing fields that spread themselves out before the hospital area. These, with British troops from the other area, assembled in their thousands and were paraded in order to be filmed, evidently for display in Japan and abroad. On two mornings, the filming was postponed owing to rain.

Week 7-14 March
A patient of mine at present at this depot, Jock Douglas, Gunner 10th Field Regiment, received a letter from his brother Bob dated 12 July from Mungallala, Queensland. Jock gave it to me to read. It was quite an unusual sensation to find oneself actually in contact with sentiments expressed in the great world outside captivity. Peter Playfair also brought news in one of his letters that Bill Woodward is married to Mary McConnel. This brought great interest to Bill Barnes, because of his

friendship with young Woodward and not less to me because of mine with the parents concerned.

On each afternoon of this weekend, troops who are going away were paraded for the usual Japanese examination 'medical'. Ten tables were placed in a row along the ground-floor verandah of this building, a medical officer in charge of each table and a line of 100 men opposite each table. This meant that 1,000 men were examined each afternoon. The number so examined, i.e. about 2,000, left us for another area, travelling by train in parties of 500 each day.

Last month, we carried out similar examinations for the remainder of the AIF that is still here.

Monday, 15 March
Bert Nimmo of Oak Park, Queensland, came out to see a gunner in the 2/15th Field Regiment. I did not know he was here. I saw him last as a schoolboy in Southport when he and his brother Bob and sister Betty all had measles. Bert showed me a letter from Mrs Campbell Kemp in which she kindly sent me a message that my people were all well. The first news I have had and a great comfort to me. I heard today there are two letters for me awaiting delivery. Jock White came and showed me a letter from his wife from Tamborine; the mountain seems now to be a mass of schools.

Tuesday, 16 March
Peter Minnett went away today; he called to say goodbye. He is a good-looking, nice-mannered fellow like his father, Roy Minnett, an old school fellow and last war associate of Eastbourne.

Also, in the morning, as the trucks were drawn up ready for departure in the Barrack Square, Dick Pockley introduced us to Bill Gaden, a fellow officer of the 2/20th Battalion whom I had not met before. A great big fellow, very pleasant and friendly, he is a son of Noel Gaden whom we used to know at Sandtofts, Ocean Street, Sydney. I heard his cousin, John Gaden is here with the 2/30th Battalion and must look him up. Dick Gaden has gone north but I am sorry I missed him.

Lieutenant-Colonel Reg White and dental officer, Jim Finimore of Ipswich, also left today. We don't know where they are all off to, possibly Bangkok, or near there.

Wednesday, 17 March
Dave Hinder went away early this morning. I shall miss him. Dick and I saw him off, jammed into the corner of a truck with 30 men. With him in the same truck went Captain Parker, son of Dr Parker of Rose Bay, Sydney.

Thursday, 18 March
A week ago I went with Alan Carrick to see Laurie West to have a midday

meal with him, only to find on arrival that he, with several other officers, were in hospital with food poisoning. The officers of the Gurkhas, having lost their men, who are held at some distant prison camp nearer Singapore City, must do their own chores. They take a month's duty at cooking in rotation: Unfortunately, Laurie West himself is the cook. However, we were entertained by Maurice Burns and young Corfield Burns the Anglo-Indian. They brought us rice and we bought a tin of pineapple cubes from them and ate our lunch in their bedroom. There has to be a strict limitation of guests at all messes on account of food supplies. Met a Captain Burnett, a very pleasant man, who had served in the 18th Battalion of the AIF in the last war; although originally from Sydney, he had been living in Malaya. (He has a dent in his head from an old bullet wound.) An officer with him showed us two six-inch guns nearby or rather the wreckage after they had been blown up by our own people last February before capitulation. The magazine was fired, it was reported that a soldier went into the magazine and threw a bomb and, of course, sacrificed himself. The wreckage was devastating. I remember hearing a colossal explosion that night at Katong seven miles from here.

Today, Captains Duncan and Millard went up north as medical officers for approximately 500 men from units of 22nd Brigade now made into one composite battalion with Ronald Campbell as CO and Major Bosley as 2 i/c.

At our Convalescent Depot eating place, we held a meeting to ask Colonel Webster to allow an Officers Mess to be formed. This was subsequently refused, but we gained permission and facilities to do private cooking in a special room and to have a Welshman, Private Stephens, as assistant cook.

There was bad news today. Ian Perry of Brisbane came to tell me that Keith Thompson had been killed. According to last news, Bill Thompson was still all right. These two brothers were at the Southport School in my time, sons of A. Thompson of Brisbane.

The other piece of sad news came from Jim Crombie who told me that David Blackstock was reported missing. I thought of him, as the only son of his poor mother.

Sunday, 21 March — Letters from Home
The greatest event of all for me — the first letter in all these months reached me — a letter from Ena at Southport dated 4 August, seven and a half months ago, was handed to me by the adjutant.

Two weeks ago we had heard the glad news that there was an arrival of mail waiting for us at the Gaol. We thought it could be weeks or even months before all mail had been censored. Such prognostication turned out to be too pessimistic. After an anxious week, letters began to arrive in camp in substantial batches. What a treasure a letter from home has become — more to be desired than gold, yea than much fine gold, more than food, more than anything, in fact, in the whole wide world.

It was to be another week before Barbara's letter (dated 29 June) and Mother's letter (dated 28 June) reached me.

The sensation I had before opening the first letter was a mixture of joyous anticipation and a kind of dread. Others amongst my friends have said they have reacted in the same way.

25 March

A lecture by Lieutenant Colonel Deakin of the 2/5th Punjab Regiment was held in the big iron-roofed shed used as the AIF theatre. The shed was packed with officers. The Battle of Slim River was the topic, or more correctly, the Battle of Telok Anson. The 12th Indian Brigade which was involved consisted of three battalions, two Indian plus the Argyle and Sutherland Highlanders. I had to leave before the end of the lecture as I had to meet Alan Carrick by appointment and go to Southern Area, where we had our evening meal with the combined officers of the Gurkha Brigade and some of the Punjab Regiment. Laurie West was our host with a young fellow from Sandhurst by the name of Dewing.

Laurie West showed us a letter from India and a snapshot of his wife and baby. He has only one baby, not twins. He had read the wireless message wrongly, and there has been such fun and chaffing about it, especially about the special dinners in honour of the twins. At the function which Alan Carrick held over at our barracks, I had waxed rather eloquent on the subject of twins, remembering my own darlings. Now it is an anticlimax for Laurie, rather pathetic in its way, but he is taking it well and is very proud of his new son even if only a singleton.

After the evening meal we repaired to the glade theatre, an open-air entertainment in Southern Area. The case of Englishmen is reinforced by one Australian, Lieutenant Colonel O'Grady of the 9th Field Ambulance. He walks all this way each evening, about two miles each way. We saw Bernard Shaw's *Androcles and the Lion;* very enjoyable and well presented. The lion was occasionally in difficulties through not being able to see well through his mask and had to be surreptitiously guided occasionally to prevent his charging over the footlights or into a wall. O'Grady was the kind-hearted Androcles who guided him. It was pleasant out under the tall trees that grow on the hillsides at this part of our picturesque prison.

Saturday, 27 March

Another 500 AIF left; they were informed only yesterday. The medical officers detailed to go with them came from the AGH. Captain John Oakshott of Lismore and Major Eddy of Melbourne.

Monday, 29 March

In the evening, went to the AIF theatre with Dick Pockley, Bill Barnes and Alan Carrick. Afterwards we ate paw paw provided by Dick.

The papaya in this country are of two varieties — one yellow inside and one red. They are occasionally on sale at the canteen, 12 cents a lb, i.e. about 50 cents for a good one.

Jim Crombie told me today that he had a son.

Tuesday, 30 March

Jock Douglass told me that Bob Neil of Surat had been killed as a pilot officer in Ceylon. I remember Bob as a boy at the Southport school: rather short and active with brown skin and eyes and very cheerful. He escaped death early in life from a perforating appendicitis. That was about 1928 when, for some weeks, he was my patient at Sandown Hospital. He was merry and good-looking, a favourite of the nurses and of most other people. It is now the war in the air, I suppose, which will rob the world of its best young men, whereas last war it was the trench warfare.

During March each of us was allowed to write a wireless message home, 24 words only.

Alan Carrick and I still enjoy our commodious quarters on the first floor. The view over the Barrack Square after six months has become somewhat monotonous for me, and the interminable noise on the concrete stairway as the men move up and down from Reveille to lights out affords one little peace. Then, again, there is a banging of beds on the different floors, a popular method of de-bugging and some, who have been lucky enough to gather firewood for their private cooking, keep it for safety in the sleeping quarters and daily chop up what they require. The 2/29th Battalion live in the building exactly opposite this one, Jim Crombie with them. The 2/26th Battalion, Queensland, live in the corner building diagonally across. Padre Polaine, Major Tracey, Captains Stan Roberts (old Southportonian), Brian Ferguson, and Schwartz, Lieutenant Gales and Lieutenant Uroe. In the near corner is the 2/30th Battalion where I recently looked for and found John Gaden. He is a company Quarter Master Sergeant and, when I found him, he was busy in a big kitchen looking tired and hot. Remembering years ago a well-groomed beau of the ball rooms of Sydney, I had a shock to see a middle-aged man. More than likely he thought me somewhat passe. In the next building to this are the West Australian machine-gunners who lost so heavily on the beaches and swamps of the west coast of this island that fatal night of 8 February when the Japanese crossed the Straits.

Wednesday, 14 April

We heard today that D Force who left in March are at Bangkok and E Force in Borneo. Major Geoff Davies is over here from the hospital for a week. This system has been introduced to give hospital people, officers and NCOs a change of scene and atmosphere. He is enjoying it immensely. More so, I think, because he so seldom leaves the hospital area. We went for a walk around the vegetable gardens this side of the road.

My batman patient (Wilkie) said Private Mudge of the 2/26th Battalion was annoyed about something today and said it was enough to make a boong swear. Boong is the Army name for our dark-skinned brothers. I knew Mudge at Caloundra camp, a fine old soldier, MM of the last war. He is generally useful and repairs boots and clogs and is the tidiest man in the 100 on the ground floor. Being short of a blanket, he spreads his bed with a Gordon kilt which I expect he acquired by bargaining in the early POW days. His kindly black face and grey whiskers look quaintly out of place with the tartan.

Thursday, 15 April
Lieutenant Baynes came up to say goodbye before going on draft. He was aide-de-camp to Sir Leslie Wilson in Brisbane for a short period. Captain Ben Barnett, the test cricketer came up, too, and Sergeant Viney from Perth and I made a bew of coffee.

In the afternoon, glass rod tests kept me going until 3.30 p.m. The people being examined are those picked for F Force which is the designation of the party going north in a few days time. There are 2,000 Australians who are to leave first in batches of 500 early each morning. After that, 5,000 British troops will begin to move from Artillery Square down in 18th Division area. Large hospital parties are to go as well; 200 from the British side of the general hospital and 200 from the Australian side. My friend, Lieutenant Colonel Huston, RAMC, is to be senior Medical Officer. With the Australian medical detachment are Major Stephens and Major Bruce Hunt, Perth, from our 13th AGH (the latter volunteered to go).

Friday, 16 April
Made some coffee at 11 a.m. for Captain Ben Barrett and Lieutenant Bob Skene. The latter is the international polo player (a nine-goal man) and comes from Campbelltown in N.S.W. Having been in India a great deal, he went there to enlist and has a commission in the Gurkha Regiment. Bob comes over here on Fridays and talks to the convalescents about polo and sometimes about Hollywood. They are apparently as interested as ever in Ben Barnett's recent talks on test cricket. This Friday evening a farewell to departing medical officers was arranged by Lieutenant Colonel Glyn White at the hospital. After the evening meal a number of us from this area walked across. The assemblage gathered in the Australian Mess Room. A contretemps occurred, the electric light failed, and all were plunged in darkness. Lamps were provided and gave a dim illumination. Colonel Galleghan gave a valedictory speech and was then followed by Glyn White. Stephens replied and then Lieutenant-Colonel Houston said a few words (he had been invited as one of the guests of honour). Supper consisted of a sandwich made of the coarse brown loaf that the hospital cook turns out, and a cup of black tea. I thought it could have been arranged on a slightly better scale.

Saturday, 17 April

For tomorrow night I have a party arranged through the good services of Sam Moffatt and Colonel Salway of the 2/26th Battalion. It is to be a gathering of soldiers of Southport and district.

Among those I have asked to come are Private Dave Gallagher: finding that he was to leave in the early hours tomorrow, he came in to say goodbye. The poor fellow looks very thin but says he is all right. He is an Englishman who migrated to Australia and has been a farmhand round Mudgeeraba and has had a hard life. These are the men to whom a greater share of the wealth of the nation should accrue.

Every Saturday evening there is a gramophone recital at the Education Centre with either David Griffin or George McNeilly (YMCA) in charge. It is pleasant to sit outside under the trees and listen for an hour or two whilst the darkness gathers and the western glow is folded in night. The sunsets here are often very lovely.

On the way across tonight to the music, I met Captain Adrian Curlewis and said goodbye to him as he likewise leaves in the morning. Though I have not seen as much of him as I would have liked, I shall miss him. He is universally liked. Jim Crombie is to leave early Monday. I have seen a lot of him as his 2/29th Battalion is just opposite our building and I shall miss him greatly. He introduced me to Graham Wilson, the Queensland Rhodes Scholar whom I have seen several times and who also leaves for the north.

Sunday, 18 April — Departure of F Force

At the early hour of 2 a.m. the first Australian party left for the far north in heavy rain, starting from the Barrack Square. Floodlights have been hung out from this building and the next which are the only two buildings out of the seven surrounding the Square which are supplied with electric light.

I was awakened by the noise of iron-shod boots on the concrete stairs, as well as of roll-calls loudly shouted in the square below, and looking over the balcony, saw the mass of men sorting themselves out, as their names were called, into little groups of 25, which assembled at different numbered posts. Most had waterproofed groundsheets round their shoulders. The remainder had none, and as the rain increased to a deluge men and baggage became drenched. I watched one man seated on his kit like a hen guarding her chickens, with his groundsheet draped to the ground like sheltering wings and underneath an old discarded bed mattress which, in all probability, was infested with bugs and had been thrown out by one of the patients on the ground floor.

As the swirling surface water rose by a couple of inches over the bitumen, the man finally rose up, gathered his belongings and made off, and as he walked away the mattress rose up and floated away in the opposite direction.

I went down our one flight of stairs to say goodbye, if possible, to

Sergeant Blackie and others whom I knew from the hospital who have had to walk over here in the middle of the night a mile or more, and then wait for two hours for the start. I found them huddled in the porch below, sheltering from the downpour, but all fairly cheery: Corporal Arthurson, Private Parker, Haines and several others.

At 4 a.m. the Japanese trucks drove into the Square with glaring lights, roaring engines, shoutings, blaring of horns. The bedraggled men scrambled aboard in the semi-darkness, each group of 25 into its own truck. In a few minutes with shouts and cries of goodwill echoed back by those few on the verandahs and balconies of these buildings, who were awake to see them go, the long file of trucks disappeared into the rain and gloom, each huddled load exposed to the full blast of the elements. Out go the lights and the Square is black and silent except for the sound of rain.

Where have they gone? It is a rail journey, that much we know. Burma? Siam? Indo-China? Many say Chang-Mai, a locality situated in North Burma at a height of over 1,000 feet. But this is pure guesswork. For some reason the Japanese keep the destination of those departed and those still to depart a closely-guarded secret.

After the midday meal I had a talk with Jim Crombie who goes tomorrow at the same early hour. He gave me a letter to his wife and I gave him a toothbrush. I shall miss him for his own sake and also because this tall western bushman reminds me constantly of dear old Tony Rowan whose friend he was.

Sunday, 18 April — Gathering of Men from Southport
This Sunday evening (Sunday before Anzac Day) is a memorable date because of this farewell gathering. I also invited to it A.G. MacAlister, Jock White, Frank Wright, and Alan Carrick.

I opened a tin of herrings and gave them two rissoles each made of herring and rice, also a slice of the brown bread made by the hospital and sold at 25 cents. A layer of dripping and salt and pepper on each slice, and plenty of black coffee sweetened with gula malacca for each man.

We sat at a long table under the electric bulb on our balcony. Wilkie, our batman, did the serving with Alan and me and he also shared in supper with us. Nineteen sat down to table, including:

26th Battalion — R. Salway, S. Moffat (Tallebudgera), Arthur Thompson (Nerang), K. Eustance, H. Watt, Bill Brooker (Springbrook), Hodson, George Riley;

30th Battalion — Sid Bignell, Vincent O'Reilly AASC, Bob Day (Surfers' Para.), Alf Russell (ordnance), A. Dean.

It was proposed that when we got home the first Sunday before Anzac Day should be the occasion for a similar gathering or reunion at the Southport Cafe. All agreed with acclamation.

The following two mornings all these men, except Alf Russell who has bad eyes, left for the north. Like the first party, they left in open trucks at 4 a.m. on the 20 mile journey to Singapore Railway Station. Fortunately the weather remained fine at the starting time each morning.

Wednesday, 21 April

The 2/30th Battalion went away during the last two or three days. I did not see John Gaden to say goodbye. I heard that Colonel Galleghan made a speech of farewell.

This afternoon I walked to the 18th Division area to say goodbye to Lieutenant Colonel Huston, RAMC. He showed me his family photographs, two boys and a little girl. I had a cup of tea with him and Lieutenant-Colonel Dillon. After leaving him I walked a little way to see a 'restaurant' which some of the Dutch troops are running. Situated in an atap hut on the side of the Changi Road, I chatted over a 5-cent cup of coffee with Captain Wallace of the British General Hospital and Mr Landals (Melbourne) of the Australian Red Cross. Wallace lives at Windermere in England and we talked a great deal. He is about 30 and is in the Indian Medical Service.

Good Friday, 23 April

The last party of the AIF F Force left at 4 a.m. today. Medical Officer Colin Jutner of Adelaide, and dental officer Mannion of Queensland accompanied them. It was fine and clear and the departure was all noise, shouting of roll calls, Australian voices, Japanese cries and orders, roaring of motor engines, greetings shouted across the Square from friend to friend, then finally the long line of glaring headlights as the trucks followed one another out of the Square. In a minute or two the sound of the last truck had died away on the Singapore road and the watchers left behind had returned to their bunks. The lonely Barrack Square was steeped again in the silence of the night. The round Easter moon looked down forever reflecting on the things that are passed away and the clock bird resumed his mournful record of the passing seconds.

That morning a party of us took a flag and walked over to the Dutch restaurant. Dick Pockley was keen to see it and brought along his friends Major Arthur Davis and Captain Owen Davis, two brothers and legal men from Sydney. In the hut, dimly lit from hurricane lamps, there was a seething crowd. Some English officers made room for us at their table. For 5 cents a piece we obtained, after a long wait, a cup of coffee and some peculiar warm lumps of jelly, slightly sweetened and coated with grated coconut, possibly made from sago flour, which can be bought at the canteen. The customers said they were very good but the average man at home would have thrown the stuff out of the window after the first bite.

Saturday, 24 April
I went to the garden area with Bill Barnes, and we met Pat Garde of Brisbane by arrangement. Pat took us, under his flag of authority, out of the main gate and down the main bitumen road to the point a quarter of a mile down the road where the main gate of the gardens is guarded by a British Military policeman on the left hand side of the road. The Japanese started these gardens last October with POW labour. The big Gaol, where 3,000 civilians are imprisoned, stands about half a mile further down on the other side of the road. From the garden area one just sees the time on the Gaol clock tower, and it is pleasant to hear its rich English chimes on the half hour.

All rubber trees have been cleared and burnt as fuel over about 90 acres. The stumps have been rooted out and the area drained and terraced. A large clean water stream runs through, coming from the big spring or 'Tong' over in the Selarang area across the road. The main vegetables grown are red spinach (amaranth), sweet potatoes, snake beans, keladi or taro root, kang-kong (green spinach) and, in the way of fruit, papaya only, although it will still need a few months before we reap the benefit of the latter. Cabbages, cauliflowers and lettuces won't grow and tomatoes, unfortunately, are not a success, neither are English potatoes or carrots. Little, if any, pumpkin is to be had, although we eat a lot of egg fruit, a kind of marrow.

Sunday, 25 April — Anzac Day
G Force went away today, silently and unfarewelled, 200 men under Major Glasgow. We heard later they had gone to Borneo to join probably the force under Major Fairlie which is already there.

The Anzac Parade was held about sundown, in front of the big Convalescent Depot building. Lieutenant-Colonel Leggatt read the well-known words 'We will remember them'. Colonel Galleghan gave an address and we had a hymn or two. It was not a very inspiring service and not like the one Lieutenant-Colonels Pigdon and Hamilton arranged at the hospital last year.

Afterwards, I went with Frank Wright to see Dick Pockley in the new house.

Monday, 26 April
In the evening there was choir practice in the hall. Afterwards we had a walk around the Barrack Square until the lights went out. Frank Wright was with me and he told me how he had come to Australia over 30 years ago with £20 in his pocket and then had secured a job with a Sydney firm within a week. He later went to Melbourne and then, after a couple of years, went into the AIF, eventually going to Egypt, Gallipoli and France.

Today, Easter Monday, the remainder of the 9th Field Ambulance becomes merged with the Convalescent Depot as the medical group.

Their dozen officers joined our Mess. There were Majors Burnside, Gunther, Watson, Park (dental), Captains Tom Mitchell (malaria officer), John Catchlove, Mr Woodruff, Alan Rogers and Mr Robb (Red Cross).

Tuesday, 27 April

Lieutenant Colonel Webster has now granted officers their own Mess and their own cook. Our service improves accordingly to an appreciable extent.

New patients arrive today under my care — Harry Smith of Soul's circus, and V.F. Johnson, the chest wound case who had such a close call last year and has now left hospital after 14 months.

Ivor Hangar's new YMCA hut was opened this afternoon. It is a bamboo atap construction opposite the RC Chapel. The AIF theatre band performed and there were some speeches.

In the evening, Major Bloom, RAMC gave a talk on the Russian Ballet. Late of Durban and London, he came over from the hospital to address us.

Sunday, 2 May

H Force, comprising 3,000 men, are going north all this week. One morning I woke at 4 a.m. and looked down into the floodlit Square and saw beneath me the Dutch troops quietly getting into trucks for their drive into Singapore to the train. Very quietly and in good order, less noisy procedures than ours: two Dutch naval officers in white uniforms and peaked caps sat at a table directly below me and nonchalantly directed operations.

Thursday, 6 May

Australians belonging to H Force are to start north next Saturday. It was to have been tomorrow but the Japanese postponed it. It includes about 600 AIF.

In the evening Alan and I had a farewell party for Dick Pockley. The gathering included Dick's friend Captain de Mowbray, former British Advisor in Trenganu. Sergeants David Griffin and Kelynack came too, also Frank Wright. Captain de Mowbray is an elderly man but was in the fighting being attached to the 22nd Brigade AIF. Dick Pockley rescued him when severely wounded by machine-gun fire in the left arm and body, and put him in a truck whereby he reached hospital. He is very tall and striking in appearance, is scholarly and idealistic as well as being a good practical man. I was told that his promotion was not as rapid as usual in the civil service because he was never a 'yes' man.

Friday, 7 May

Dick Pockley is to leave with his party of H Force tomorrow. With his usual generosity he has brought me gifts the last few days, things to add to my reserve; items which he 'can't carry', e.g. a tin of bacon, a tin of soup, and a little helping of marmite out of his last tin, a hat and a pair of shoes.

This evening went to the lawn under the casuarina trees by the main building to listen to the music with Dick and the Davis brothers who are also to leave tomorrow. An hour after dark the program had ended so I walked back with the others to their house and kept them company as they ate their breakfast — their last meal here — at 11 p.m. Colonel Oakes, their Commanding Officer, sat opposite. I then left them and went to bed.

Saturday 8 May

I slept through the din of departure. At 10 to 4 Dick dashed up the stairs and woke me saying 'we are off now'. I followed him down in my sleeping clothes which, these days, consist of a singlet and a tattered nether garment, a towel or whatnot, and I clattered in wood clogs across the Square on his trail. There was just time to shake dear old Dick by the hand. In the kindness of his heart he had let me sleep to the last moment. The Jap guard shouted something meaning, 'How many men aboard the truck?' and Dick counted heads rapidly and shouted back 'Ni ja go' (25) and then, with a few departing shouts, they were off into the darkness of the great unknown, and thus I have lost another friend from Selarang and the most generous and kindly of them all. On other truck loads I found Russell Braddon and Hugh Moore and gave them farewell as they too started off.

Sunday, 9 May

My happy home for the last 7 months is finally to be broken up today as Rickety Kate tells me we are both to go. Alan Carrick is to leave the Convalescent Depot, preparatory to going away with the next party, and I am to move a floor higher up to join the other medical officers of the new composite unit.

In the afternoon, I walked with David Griffin across the road to the old 11th Division area to see Captain de Mowbray. We chatted in the porch of an atap hut under the shade of rubber trees with a distant view of the sea. It had a peaceful and countrified air after the clatter of the Barrack Square and there were ducks quacking contentedly round about. The Captain gave us a cup of black tea each, and what was very hospitable, a fairly ripe banana each.

Monday, 10 May

I moved up to the top floor at the other end, back to Alan Carrick's first billet where we had a week together at the time when Dutch Headquarters turned me out. Lovely view from the balcony, so I risked the chance of rain beating in and avoided the crush inside the room.

Majors K. Burnside and Gunther and Captain Tom Mitchell are in the little room beside me. It's nice to be near Tom with his multitudinous studies and cheerful talk.

Tuesday, 11 May
In the evening there was a lecture in the Depot Hall by Lieutenant Colonel D'Anboz on Italy.

Wednesday, 12 May
In the evening I went with Alan Carrick to the house across the valley now occupied by the Gurkha officers. I saw Laurie West there and listened to Colonel D'Anboz give a talk on the Battle of Britain (August 1940-March 1941).

Afterwards, we were given a drink of home-brewed hooch which nearly made me vomit and kept Padre Quirk awake all night.

Friday, 14 May
Colonel D'Anboz gave an address on France. These lectures are popular, so it is a packed house, the heat would incubate eggs.

Saturday, 15 May
Alan Carrick came early, about 7 a.m., to tell me that J Force (Lieutenant Colonel Byrnes) is leaving today at about 3 p.m. and he was going with him as adjutant. Also going is Major Ron Campbell, ex-2/40th Battalion, Alan's friend. They are to go overseas. Several of my patients are going: my batman, Wilkie of Queensland, and Sapper Bourne, the very thin man. Captain Boyce from Queensland and Major Murray and Captain Nairnsey are the medical officers, the last two from BGH. Major (Lord) d'Ramsay was also to have gone with the party (his sister is reported to be the wife of the French Ambassador at Tokyo), much to Alan's delight as he derives amusement out of the idea of having a 'belted earl' under his command.

The party were issued later in the morning with woollen pullovers and balaclavas so they must be going to Japan or somewhere near it. Everybody appeared in great spirits now and are very optimistic. Alan came to us for lunch and then had to bolt back to catch his truck on the Square at 2 p.m. I bolted after him and saw him off, so seeing off another friend, a good stablemate and the most sociable light-hearted and amusing person I have met in these parts.

I have been given orders to return to AGH on Monday. I conceived the idea that I would like to be included in garden party quarters for a change before going back to wards and sick people, so walked over to see Major Maxwell and Pat Garde who were very friendly and agreeable to having me there.

Sunday, 16 May
Went to AIF Headquarters early, and saw Lieutenant Colonel Leggatt who was very nice and said he would recommend my going to a garden party.

After evening service there was music outside the YMCA hut. After that we went to 'Smokey Joe's', the restaurant opened by the Dutch and then taken over by the Army. Laurie West and Maurice Burns were there; they are all going tomorrow. One wonders how many will eventually be left at Selarang!

Tonight, in the intense heat and sweaty crowd of half-naked humanity, we are being very merry over cups of terribly inferior coffee, and the deafening din of voices competes with a powerful and tireless pianist pounding out jazz-time non stop.

Monday, 17 May

The officers' party left today. Two hundred and forty British and 60 Australians left in drizzling rain at midday. Nice debonair young Peter Playfair is going with them. I said goodbye and was sorry to see him depart. Also, amongst the Indian Army officers leaving were Laurie West, Corfield, Dewing and Maurice Burns. This party is considered part of H Force but is reported to be going north only for three months and then returning here, but nobody believes this.

At evening Mess, Padre Quirk had the Dutch Chaplain-in-Chief to eat with us. He is a brother of the Dutch Commander in Chief interned in Holland. He told me the name of the Dutch Governor-General in Java at the time of surrender, Tjalda van Starkenborg Stachouwer.

Today is Frank Wright's birthday. He opened a tin of curried chicken at Mess and kindly shared it with me, then we celebrated further by walking to the hospital with the party going to the Palladium Theatre. After some difficulty with Padre Wearne, the door keeper, the difficulty was resolved when I whispered in his ear that it was Frank's birthday. We were given good seats and saw the wild and merry *Max's Revels*. After the show Frank had the bright idea of going backstage to congratulate Captain McGeraghty, the producer, which we duly did.

Tuesday, 18 May

I moved to the garden party quarters today with my new old batman driver Eldridge. Sergeant Jack Ryan came over with us to help with the trailer and with my gear. He touched me very much by presenting me with a little farewell address done up in the form of a book marker. I took a bed, also, for Eldridge.

I saw Sergeant Lancaster of Beaudesert at the ordnance-depot and he helped me to obtain a pair of new boots for Eldridge. These are as rare as diamonds these days. Our good luck was partly due to the fact that he takes five and so small a size is seldom in demand.

I saw young Piddington, the conjurer, today and was glad to know he had not been sent north. Piddington was a pupil of Keith Lumsdaine at Sydney Grammar School and thinks a great deal of him.

The garden group is a composite unit of mixed Australian and British. They live in a row of two-storied houses facing the main Changi Road just inside the barbed-wire fence; the houses were once occupied by warrant officers of the Garrison troops, the Gordon Highlanders, and their families. Opposite is the padang or playing field in the 11th Division area. We face south and so get the prevailing breezes at this time of year — soft little puffs of wind as if propelled by some punkah-wallah who occasionally dozes. A couple of miles, away across the tops of rubber trees and palms, one sees patches of the hazy tropic sea. Very occasionally a large steamer appears on the horizon, or a native prau, but mostly there is nothing.

I share a room with Captain Ian McGregor of Toowoomba and ex-11th Light Horse Regiment and two Englishmen of the 2nd Gurkha Regiment, Captain Kemmiss Batty and Captain Alec Ogilvey of Calcutta. The latter knew Sir Leslie Wilson's family well in Berkshire. In our flat, also, are Major Maxwell, Pat Garde, and Lieutenant John Meillon of Mosman, Sydney. Others are Australians: Captain Burnett Schulte, Brisbane; Tom Bunning, W.A.; Michael Manor (Malayan Civil Service Mersing attached AIF). The British are Major Harvard (18th Division Artillery) and Coleman, Captains Dick Frampton (Malayan Agricultural Department), Bob Darby, Vandeguecht, Fred Cross (mountain artillery, Indian Army) Warrington and Scott Russell.

Wednesday, 19 May

I spent the morning in the gardens with Major Maxwell and Sergent Willesey, ex-planter, planting papaya seedlings. In the evening a small affable Japanese soldier came and squatted in a cane chair beside me in front of our quarters and offered to buy watches or fountain pens.

Thursday, 20 May

Owing to heavy rain, no-one worked in the garden today. The vegetable gardens date from October last year and a great deal of work has been done. Each officer has his own area and there are a few permanent gardeners to each, but most of the workers report daily for duty from their units in the Barrack Square. There is still a sentry on duty at the main gate but he knows those of us who belong to the garden group, or most of us. In any case, we walk out freely on to the main road whenever we want to do so, down the half mile of 'freedom' until one enters the garden main gate and so into an enclosed wired-in area again. There are acres of tapioca and keladi (taro root) but the main produce is spinach of different varieties and sweet potatoes. The leaves of the latter are cropped three times a week and three truckloads as a rule go to the POW camp and to the hospital. Many sweet potatoes are also being dug up and supplied now; also the long snake beans are bearing plentifully. There is a large coconut tree grove in the centre, a pleasant and cool spot — the trees rise to a great height. Other fruits are rare, unfortunately; a few mangosteens and cachounuts, the fruit of which are very juicy and rather nice but one only rarely finds them. The planted papaya trees are growing in hundreds but will not be bearing for some

months. Visiting this rather pleasant spot daily, after lunching in the tent
à la picnic at midday and working just as much or as little as I please,
I found the next six weeks passed all too quickly. A strange contrast
to one's usual attitude to prisoner-of-war life.

Two afternoons a week I visited the English Officers Mess at the
hospital to hear Colonel Taylor lecture on surgery. I enjoyed the walk
along Changi Road, so shady and restful with some lovely trees.

The cemeteries are looking trim and peaceful, being well kept by our
soldiers. First the AIF cemetery standing back a little from the road,
then the larger British cemetery with its hundreds of wooden crosses lined
correctly as if on their last parade. On three or four occasions I also visited
friends at the AGH, having a cup of tea with them, and Major Proctor
kindly gave me some necessary dental treatment.

Friday, 21 May

All day was spent in the gardens with Major Maxwell planting out papaya
seedlings. The seedlings are grown at a large, unoccupied Chinese house
on the hill where the basement has been converted into a nursery under
the care of an Australian, Staff Sergeant White, ex-manager of
Needlewood Station somewhere near Moree in N.S.W. — a particularly
nice fellow.

Working in the sun in this country is not dangerous but one becomes
drenched with sweat in a few minutes, hence the wearing of scanty
clothes. The men wear usually hats, boots and loinclothes of some kind;
the officers wear an ancient pair of shorts. Those wearing glasses must
wear a sweat rag around the forehead to avoid becoming blinded. I have
found the sun glasses I bought in Sydney a Godsend.

Of the troops here, one out of every three nowadays has eye trouble
or has had it. It began about last August after six months of imprisonment
— keratitis — ascribed to a deficiency of vitamin B2. A few of these
developed corneal ulcers with resulting blindness. Then, later, retro-
bulbar-neuritis (optic nerve inflamation with consequent blind spots or
'scotomata'). Fortunately, the type occurring here has not led on to
blidness but most cases have slowly responded to treatment in the form
of extra rice polishings, yeast and, as far as possible, marmite. The latter
gave out some months back and, since the Japanese ceased to give us
sugar, the yeast is not very palatable so the patients have to eat about
a mugful of rice-polishings which is about as tasty as a similar amount
of pollard!

Added to these daily afflictions, a new one has been introduced in the
last four months in the form of a 'soup' made from couch grass and wild
passionfruit. This soup gives extra vitamin B.

For weeks and months, those with the eye problem are unable, or not
allowed, to read. Dark glasses are hard to procure and cost over a dollar
at the canteen so not all can afford them, and hence have to keep indoors
out of the glare. They seem to be consoled by one another's company

and they yarn and play cards. The music and the lectures at the Convalescent Depot Hall and other places by the YMCA men and the Education Centre team are a Godsend to many of these unfortunates. They are cheerful for the most part but the idle, inactive life cannot be other than detractive of initiative and self-reliance in the case of the youngsters. There is nothing much they can do except make brooms and clogs when allowed some work. Of later months, those with sunglasses are allowed light work in the gardens.

One morning, in the gardens, I sat at the gate on the west side, i.e. that side of the garden which is flanked by the Tanamara Road and chatted with the sentry, an English soldier of the Manchester Regiment who told me his wife and child are in the Gaol and that he has not seen or heard of them since Christmas. He always hopes to see them some day passing along the road. The Gaol prisoners, women and children, have, at rare intervals, been seen under Sikh guards going for a walk or for a bathing excursion to the beaches.

Whilst I talked with the sentry, a trailer party of European men prisoners, about six or eight in number, went past pushing their load. They passed within a few feet and looked fairly fit but one could only say 'good day' as they passed, as their Sikh guard was with them. One man winked at me and smiled cheerfully, it provided a small interest to the morning as also did the sight of an elderly Englishman prisoner across the road who had come down from the Gaol, accompanied by the Sikh guard as usual stalking just behind him. The Englishman appeared to be an engineer, his morning work appearing to be the inspection of, and attention to, a pumping engine situated in a small engine house opposite to where we were squatting.

An Australian Officers Club was inaugurated at the end of May, situated on the ground floor of a large house beside AIF Headquarters. Here we can foregather in the evenings (only) and buy a cup of black coffee for 2½ cents and a piece of something to eat with it in the shape of a doover which is the term in current use for nondescript lumps of edible substance made from rice, maize or sago flour or gula malacca and coconut. The Dutch officer attached to the Club, van der Mata, is, like many Dutch, a cook of imagination and resourcefulness. Sometimes his peanut cake is available and is really good. On the weekend nights there is often music, either by the AIF Theatre Party Orchestra or by the Orchestra and entertainers from the Palladium which is the big theatre over at the hospital. As Colonel Galleghan said in his remarks on the opening night of the Club, it is good to have a common meeting place and to be able there to extend hospitality to our friends in the British forces.

Sunday, 13 June
At 7 p.m. I arrived at the top floor of the hospital building which contains the C Mess of the BGH and dined with Wallace, also Clancy, the American Red Cross man and Landals of the Australian Red Cross.

Amongst other guests were Captains Smith-Ryan (Perth) and Kinder, ex-Malay Police. Our three-course meal included a little tinned salmon — I had seen no tinned meat or fish for at least four months, so it was a treat.

Afterwards we sat on the roof and enjoyed the air and the lovely view.

Wallace comes from Windermere beside the Lake; I recalled the days spent there at Storrs Hall Hotel with Ena in 1920. He is a kindly, thoughtful man, free of all affectation and mannerisms, and with a voice that is very pleasant to listen to, and an idealism which one would not necessarily expect in a young and good-looking officer of the Regular Army.

Saturday, 19 June
Lieutenant-Colonel Glyn White told me he wants me to leave my present quarters on Wednesday and go to do Captain Catchlove's job as RMO to C Group. This means going back to live in the Barrack Square. C Group is a unit of about 350 and comprises the relics of all of our infantry personnel including a few of the 2/4th Machine Gunners.

Catchlove is going away with another all-medical party.

Monday, 21 June
After the lecture at the hospital I met Clancy and Wallace by arrangement and we went for a swim in the disused swimming bath of the Garrison area. Colonel Strachan and another medical officer happened to go by and reminded us of the dangers of a leptosporosis infection, but these seemed remote when we looked at the cool water in the tiled bath. Clancy did some very fancy dives off the high tower.

Wednesday, 23 June
After a pleasant six weeks with the gardeners, I moved across to the Barrack Square. I shall miss my room-mates, Ian McGregor, Alec Ogilvey, Peter Kemmiss. My batman, 'Sailor' Eldridge, wants to stay here. I tried to arrange it for him but was not able to.

'Sailor' helped me pack with the aid of Churchill and another man and we pushed my gear across to the Square on a trailer. The new quarters are on the top floor of the third-storey block. After getting my stuff up the stairs I sent the three perspiring boys for a drink at Smokey Joe's, the Dutch canteen, at my expense.

My new quarters are on the top floor with 14 other Australian officers right opposite and one floor higher from where Alan Carrick and I used to live.

Friday, 25 June
Today is a sad day because my old friend Geoff Davies is going away tonight as also is my more recent friend, Captain E.H. Wallace. Others to go are Eddy Marshall and the elderly dentist from the BGH.

Eddy is 53 years of age and if he or the dental officer die of illness or maltreatment up north, it may be that the British medical authorities here will be responsible. It is true that a certain number of medical men have to be sent, but to select a man of Marshall's age and physique in preference to younger, or more popular or privileged men, is to show not only partiality in selection of medical officers but also indifference to the welfare of those troops whom such selected MOs are being sent to look after. The latter troops are our own prisoners of war who have previously been sent north and who may be living under worse conditions than we know and who, in any case, will be getting far less healthy conditions then we are getting here.

Geoff Davies volunteered to go, but I wish our ADMS had sent the other pathologist and retained dear old Geoff who only volunteered out of a certain spirit of service.

This evening it was, of course, dark and drizzling in the Barrack Square. At about 9.30 p.m. we gathered to wish them farewell as they crowded into their trucks, about 25 to a truck which made the sides bulge. Poor old Geoff was loaded down with too much luggage; I hope he won't have to jettison any. We waved good-bye and the trucks moved off in line out of the Square, reminiscent of so many other goodbyes on the same spot.

Sunday, 11 July
A man of the AIF named E. Allen of Dural, Sydney, was buried in the cemetery here today by Padre Barratt. Allen died in solitary confinement in Outram Gaol in Singapore, one of the minor tragedies of war. Two of our officers were sent from here to the Gaol to see him but found only his body in his cell, very wasted. The Japanese say he died of beri-beri.

Monday, 19 July
Went to the Officers' ward and saw both MacAlisters. Young MacAlister had just arrived at the hospital after many months in Outram Gaol, Singapore. I hardly recognised him but his mind is quite clear. I only stayed a few minutes with him according to orders from the Medical Officer in charge. I asked him what he would like to eat, and he replied 'a bag of sugar'.

Thursday, 22 July
This afternoon I asked Major Orr to test my eyesight which has deteriorated and which he cheerfully told me will go on deteriorating until I am 60! I was hoping that part, at least, of the defect was due to the climate and the glare and lack of meat, etc, in the diet. I am now only 8 stone 13 lbs and seem to stick at that. I have to wear both my glasses at once in order to read or to thread a needle. Following on the latter complaint, I qualify for a new pair of glasses from Singapore. The Red

Cross representatives have been able to arrange to obtain a limited number of prescription glasses from an oculist in Singapore. These are only supplied to special cases. In my case, fortunately for me, new glasses are considered necessary for medical work.

Friday, 23 July
Bill Barnes gave a birthday party this evening at the Officers' Club to which about six of us repaired and drank coffee and ate doovers at Bill's expense.

Sunday, 25 July
I called over to the Gurkha Officers in the afternoon to see Major Robertson and had a long chat with him about various topics, including local songbirds.

The Americans have recently proved good pals to our troops. Here and elsewhere mixed baseball is popular and going well. It appears a good game.

Monday, 26 July
Every day or two there is an issue of fish to our group (360 men) — allowance is 80-90 lbs, and is supplied by the Japanese Army. I have to inspect our allotment at the Supply Depot along the road near the canteen before issue. The stuff generally consists of a pile of little sweep or similar miniature fish and the weight includes everything — scales, bones, heads, tails and guts. Many of them are too small to clean. Occasionally there are small sharks, 1-2 feet long, catfish, or a steak of stingray or skate. The latter grow to a good size in these waters; the flesh is reddish and repulsive to see raw, but not bad in the eating. However, it comes so seldom that in the six weeks I have been here the Officers Mess has only had stingray once and, on that occasion, it was so impregnated with ammonia that I could not eat my piece. (The ammonia comes from a leak in the pipes at the freezing plant in Singapore; the ice absorbs the ammonia and then imparts it to the fish which is kept cool by pieces of chopped ice on the trip out here.)

The Japanese check parade continues each evening as usual, about 7 p.m. We are checked always by the same NCO who must be as sick of it as we are. His expression is a mixture of boredom and slight malaise, but he returns our salute courteously enough as they all do. His embarrassment, if it be such, I imagine is due partly to the fact of facing 350 foreigners alone and partly to a little sword trouble which he has while walking up to our part. Their swords are badly hung on any kind of belt and they swing about and threaten to trip the wearer as he walks along. Whilst we fall in on one part of the road, a large party of British troops fall in on the Barrack Square nearby and, beside them, another party of 300 Dutch. There are too few Americans here (12 men and 3 officers) to make a special parade so I imagine they fall in with the British troops.

I am quite used to these tropical climes and never imagined life on the equator was so cool.

Thursday, 29 July

I had a day out with Bob Skene who was on the wood party. Starting at 9 a.m. we walked along through the prison gate, passed the school where dozens of native children, well dressed and well cared for, as far as one could gauge from a distance of 50-100 yards, were playing under and around the neat school house. We passed some others walking to school further down the road and the Malay schoolmaster, a young and rather flash-looking fellow, with hair well oiled and wavy and a blue shirt with khaki shorts and stockings and tan shoes.

At the Japanese guardhouse we had to wait about 20 minutes for their changing-of-the-guard 'ceremony'. The new guard marched up and broke into a German goose step as they approached. The old guard turned out to meet them. The two lines faced each other, but instead of our ceremony of presenting arms, etc., there was much shouting and bowing on the part of the NCOs in charge. After this the new guard filed into the hut and the sergeant sat on the verandah and received the passes and the obeisances of the various natives who passed by, Malays or Chinese. When our turn came, we saluted as we passed the guard house and wheeled to the right. A little further the bitumen road topped a rise, then our entire party mounted on our particular trailer and we coasted downhill for about one mile, reaching a speed which must have been not less than 35 miles an hour, all rather hair-raising on account of the precarious hold one had on the swaying bodies on the flat-topped vehicle.

We cut out rubber trees and grubbed out stumps and, at lunchtime, fed a clutch of chickens with rice; a fine clutch of about 18, belonging to a Chinese farmhouse 20 yards away. These little farmhouses look very bare and poverty-stricken. Later on, as we grubbed out stumps, two Chinese girls, one with bobbed hair, working at their crops about 50 yards away, were giggling and showing off before the Tommies of our party. I was afraid they might get into trouble from the Japanese guards, who stand around with their rifles, but the latter either did not notice or were not concerned.

Sunday, 1 August

I had my evening meal with the garden group. We sat on the lawn afterwards and listened with interest to Australian aviator, Squadron Leader Matheson, one of the seven who were captured in Burma early this year. After capture they were taken down the Irrawaddy to Rangoon, then flown across some time later to Bangkok where they spent one night, and thence by the same plane to Singapore Island. On arrival, they were sent to Changi Village near here, but for some reason we do not know they were kept apart from the rest of the POWs for the next three or four months.

Monday, 2 August

Bob Skene gave a talk on international polo at the gymnasium building, which is also fitted up and used by the English Chaplain Young as a church. Bob lent nonchalantly on the lectern, looking like a fair-skinned Rajah Prince, and gave a very interesting talk. Those present were mostly British Officers with a few AIF.

Tuesday, 3 August

There is a rumour of further mail bags at the Gaol and, from then on, I could think of little else.

Friday, 6 August

We had a cricket match in front of the Convalescent Depot in the afternoon. I always think cricket would be a better game if one were allowed to be let off the first time out, i.e. provided one has only amassed a run or two up to the moment of the first collapse. I never seem able to make more than 5 or 6 runs and then spend hours waiting in the sun whilst others enjoy themselves making 30 or 40 runs.

As we finished, Tony Newsom hailed me from the verandah waving a letter, and my heart gave a great leap. It was from May Ponsford, God bless her, and gave me great pleasure. It was dated 3 October from Taunton, Devon, and it came in its own envelope, addressed by her to Red Cross, Tokyo; not in the official Red Cross envelope. Tony Newsom and Alec Downer and others go each day to the Gaol to sort letters. There are only about a couple of thousand AIF letters and those that have arrived appear to be a hangover from the mail we got last March, the only mail we have had. Most of the letters are dated July and August 1942, and the latest from Australia of which I have heard was 26 October 1942. I shall go on hoping for a day or two for letters from home.

Saturday, 7 August

There are reports that the whole hospital is to move to 11th Division area which has taken until now to cleanse after the natives went. There are also reports that troops from this Barracks will go to Singapore, Johore Bahru or some other place on the near mainland. One hopes it will all remain a rumour as it is all very disturbing.

Sunday, 8 August

I went alone to early service at the volunteer regiments' quarters. Van de Gucht and Captain Hodman were also there. The bearded and venerable Major Petter of Kuala Lumpur held his usual impressive service in the little room.

Monday, 9 August

I have given up hope of any letters from home by this present distribution. How many more months of waiting?

Tuesday, 10 August

There is a cholera scare in Singapore, so all drinking water from the town supply is to be chlorinated. For the two buildings here we have the tank part of a water cart trailer and a couple of 40 gallon petrol drums.

Last week I attended an entertainment given by the Dutch in the AIF theatre. The place was packed, which must mean about 800 I should think. It was a musical comedy about two young bloods touring the world. They were smart, well-groomed and clever, and the female impersonators were good. One of the latter, in fact, was quite ravishing in a long, blue evening gown, blonde, beautiful and languorous.

Although given in Dutch, we could get the theme and the occasional joke. I was sitting with Smith-Ryan, and next to him sat a Dutch officer who helped a little with translation.

Wednesday, 11 August

I went to Smokey Joe's restaurant with Ian McGregor and brought away a couple of Changi cakes to eat later. Quite good, but 7 cents a piece is rather expensive.

In the afternoon, I walked across to one of the houses over near the Gurkhas headquarters to see Captain de Mowbray, and enjoyed a cup of tea and an hour's talk with him. I provided the cakes purchased this morning. I wanted to hear from him about the medical facilities in Trangani State where he was a British adviser. Trangani State has 400,000 inhabitants, but only one small hospital and a lay doctor before the war. Apparently, it is a very poor State and the Malays do not take to Western medicine.

One of the objects of my visit this afternoon was to ask after the Captain's health because I noticed at last Monday night's class that he looked very sick and anaemic and his feet swollen. Our diet, which to all intents and purposes is wholly vegetarian, seems to affect men in their 60s (as he must be) rather severely.

This evening I was invited for the evening at 6.15 p.m. with the convalescent officer patients. Lieutenant Colonel Wright, my host, had been sent today to the hospital with dysentery, so Major Proctor and Padre McNeil, both old soldiers, took his place and looked after me. Bill Dolamore took the President's place.

Our three-course meal started with toragay soup and ended with a sweet of sliced banana and sago jelly with grated coconut. We toasted the King in coffee sweetened with gula malacca. Major Proctor told me afterwards how they distilled alcohol at the hospital from sweet potato, gula malacca and yeast.

Later in the evening I went to a meeting of the Mountain Club. Tom Mitchell is President, and we listened to a talk on a hike in Sikkim made by a Dutch officer, Dr Klompe (geologist). He did a round walk from Darjeeling, over 100 miles.

Thursday, 12 August

I was on the roof before breakfast this morning where I usually go for a run and exercises, followed by a rest in the fresh morning air to watch the sun rise once again. This morning there was a fishing fleet of praus and junks well out to sea; the first occasion I have seen a number out at one time. Perhaps the Japanese are allowing the natives now to go further out to fish owing to the cholera scare in Singapore.

This evening Smith-Ryan and Norman Paul and I went to the AIF theatre, a rattling good show. Harry Smith excelled himself as a dowager, passé but distinguée, in a lovely gown, faultless coiffure and ruby earrings. He sang an old-fashioned melody. Young Piddington mystified the house with conjuring tricks, completely baffling two ragged soldiers in shorts who volunteered to go up from the audience and were made to look silly hunting for an egg in a handbag. Piddington has a charm of manner, in spite of his slight stutter, which makes him very popular.

The usual commedienne, Jack Smith, is performing at the Palladium at present. His place was taken by Capell, ex-Field Ambulance orderly, and was very clever. My old patient, Brightfield, gave a solo on his xylophone.

Friday, 13 August

The breeze from the south freshened to quite a continuous fanning which made last night delightfully cool and I slept all night with a blanket.

At 4 p.m. I joined K. Betty and Fred Cross at the YMCA hut and listened to the New World Symphony on the gramophone. Ivor Hangar played it and George McNeilly and young Cross of the East Surreys explained, as we went along, to the audience. About 20 or 30 turned up to hear it.

The general restlessness which followed the announcement of a probable move from this prison area seems to be dying down as it becomes more probable that we shall stay here. For this, everybody is hopeful and profoundly thankful.

Saturday, 14 August

Today the blow fell but not as severely as was expected. The news has come of an order from the Japanese that the whole hospital, British and Australian, is to come over here to the Barrack Square, and the troops here are to move to another part of Selarang area. Nobody wants to move but, on the other hand, there is general relief that there has been no order threatening a removal of troops to some other distant prison camp as we feared at first.

All connected with the hospital must be glad that the move to the hut encampment over the main road is now definitely cancelled. I personally am pleased because Glyn White has told me that I am to rejoin the hospital when it comes over to the Barrack Square.

The AGH will move into this building and the next, that is back to where it started after the capitulation; this time, thank God, without all the poor, suffering, suppurating wounded men. The last wounded man left hospital some time ago, though many have to be readmitted from time to time for further operations.

Sunday, 15 August
I went to see A.G. MacAlister who is still a patient, returned to Selarang and then went to Church in the AIF theatre to Padre Barrett's service for C Group. It's a pity more men don't attend for he preaches a fine sermon. I am afraid the officers don't set a good example in the way of attendance.

Monday, 16 August
The quality of this notebook, bought at the canteen for 36 cents, speaks for itself. The price of almost everything is rising. Gula malacca is now 66 cents a pound so that many people prefer to buy sugar, which is more plentiful and which costs 85 cents. Eggs are seldom available and, when they are, the cost is 25 cents, which is prohibitive.

Today is the big move away from Barrack Square to make room for the combined hospital which is coming across from Roberts Barracks. Captain George McLaughlin, 2/18th Battalion, and Norman Morrison, 2/29th Battalion, moved their companies across to-day.

There are four houses available over near AIF Headquarters near the hospital gate. In their new quarters, a two-roomed house, each company seems quite happy although the rooms are crowded and their sad-looking home-made beds are almost touching.

Tuesday, 17 August
The rest moved across today and left me almost alone on the vast empty top floor. Jack Dole, the Quartermaster, remained, and he and I and the two cooks had the evening meal together in the kitchen.

A young soldier named Quinn developed acute osteomyelitis of the shine bone following a hit with the cricket bat and I sent him to the hospital today.

In the evening I went to the Palladium Theatre to see the new show known as *The Little Admiral*. After the show the rain had cleared and we walked home in the moonlight.

Wednesday, 18 August
All alone except for Dixon and Forsyth of the AGH, who have come over as advance party.

In the evening I attended a meeting of the Mountain Club; Captain Tom Mitchell was in the chair.

From today until next Monday evening, 23 August, I have my meals at the Officers Mess of the Convalescent Depot whilst waiting the arrival of the hospital.

Monday, 23 August

The fall of Sicily has been announced in *Syonan Times*.

Tonight I had my first meal with the hospital Officers' Mess, thus rejoining the hospital after an absence of nearly 11 months. A lot has happened since then.

This evening, Captain Greener of the Entertainment Committee of the Convalescent Depot, arranged a talk at the AIF theatre hall, the Convalescent Depot hall being filled up with troops now. A Rajput Officer and a young Captain Earle gave addresses on the fighting in Burma which took place when the 14th Division invaded there at the end of last year. The Indian Officer is a fine-looking chap and I admired his pluck in giving the talk as his English was not too good.

Tuesday, 24 August

I have been put in charge of a medical ward on the first floor and have arranged to be in the bed beside Carl Furner on the balcony. We are well packed in, but still quite comfortable as long as the rain does not come in this way.

In the late afternoon I found young Flight Lieutenant MacAlister in the skin ward downstairs. I was shocked to see how ill he still is, his face and legs bloated with oedema, muscles all wasted and weak, and skin covered with a blotchy irritative rash. He is very anxious for visitors now.

After the evening meal I walked over to the woodcutters' group (Bob Skene's men) at his invitation to hear young Flying Officer Bagot speak. He and Jensen are the two American flying officers in camp. They were part of the crew of a Liberator which had been shot down in Burma on 31 March this year. (When they went to India last year, after a year's training, they flew there in seven days from the States via Africa.)

Wednesday, 25 August

The last member of the hospital Officers Mess arrived over today. The British side of the hospital is still in the thick of the move.

Departure of L Party Up-country

An all-medical party sent up as reinforcements somewhere, some say to a camp near Bangkok, today. The Japanese never tell us where the parties are going. The Party consisted of about 12 British medical officers and three Australians: Major Lyle Andrews in charge, with Tom Crankshaw and Murphy, also 70 Australian other ranks and 30 British. They left just after midnight and the night was black as pitch but fortunately with no rain.

Thursday, 26 August

From now on the hospital is established again into the first buildings into which we moved nearly 18 months ago. The first months were, of course, the worst when the wounded were suffering most and many of them dying and when, in the black months of March and April, the dysentery raged at its height.

My ward now is named 3A, on the ground floor of building 173, and my Ward Sergeant is a good man named Shelton, an Englishman by birth, who came to Australia just after the last war.

Most of the 70 patients are convalescing and there is little to do.

Saturday, 28 August
I heard today that there are 40 bags of mail at the Gaol, two of which are for the AIF. This means some thousands of letters. What joy to anticipate. Already yesterday, Major Bert Nairn and young Ivan Mackay had Red Cross card messages from home and were allowed by the Japs to reply, the reply being handed in to the Orderly Room. This perhaps begins a new era.

This Saturday evening I met Austin Edwards as usual to listen to the program of gramophone music at the Convalescent Depot. A larger crowd than usual. Many of the Dutch seem quite old men with white beards. A great number attend without shirts, in their daytime garb, not seeming to feel the cool evening air.

We all went along afterwards to the Officers Club and had a cup of coffee and a 'Changi coconut jelly'.

Sunday, 29 August
Just finishing Winston Churchill's *Into Battle*, his speeches of 1938, 1939 and 1940. Faith, love of country, constancy, courage, prophecy and all enshrined in faultless English. One would like to be able to quote whole paragraphs from each speech.

Wednesday, 1 September
There is a wide and pleasant view across to the Straits on the left and the now deserted Roberts Barracks to the right. Since the hospital left the latter the other day, the buildings still appear empty and unoccupied by the Japanese.

At 8 p.m. I went to the meeting of the Mountain Club where Lieutenant Rawlins, brother of Margaret Rawlins, the English actress, gave a talk on mountaineering in Japan. He lived there and taught in a school. He is a highly-strung, nervous person with a bad stammer. He graphically described the sensation of standing on the lip of a crater and seeing the eruption of red hot rocks hurtling 3,000 feet into the air (or was it 300 feet?).

Thursday, 2 September
The C of E Chaplains of the hospital have constructed a small chapel under some palm trees on the western side of the Square. Tonight Padre Pain invited me and Bob Dick and Carl Furner to a social evening outside

the chapel. There were tables and chairs under the trees and a new moon. About 20 orderlies and a few officers were present beside ourselves, including Padre Chambers, the Acting Chaplain General. There were songs to a harmonium and a 'squeeze box' and the spirit of good cheer was enhanced by a supper of Towgay savouries, followed by coconut 'lamingtons'. Padre Chambers gave a humourous recitation or rather monologue.

Friday, 3 September
I went to early Communion at 8.30 a.m. (Padre Wearne) and in the evening attended the AIF Theatre with some of our officers and saw a very cheery program.

Sunday, 5 September
A general parade of all AIF units or what is left of them here. Church service was at 10 a.m. in the theatre hall with about 700 or 800 present.

The sermon was good, the subject being the spirit that has carried the Empire through the crisis. But I found the Padre, as usual, uninspiring, too timid and apologetic, without the fire that one expects and for which one craves when one thinks of the lives that have been given for our cause and the heroism that has, in countless cases, been so apparent and so much in contrast to that soul-destroying, lethargic, prudent, safety-first philosophy of the 1930s. The hymns were 'Oh God our Help in Ages Past', 'Fight the Good Fight' and 'Abide with Me'. It was very moving to hear men sing as the troops sang on this occasion. Afterwards we formed up outside by units and then marched past the Commander, Colonel Galleghan. The AIF theatre band provided an inspiring military march.

Monday, 6 September
Some thousands of letters are being sorted at the Gaol. The word is that there are several thousand for the AIF so we are all living in hope and excitement.

Tuesday, 7 September
In the little atap hut this side of the Convalescent Depot, which the YMCA fellows built, are now held afternoon and evening meetings of all kinds.

This afternoon George McNeilly gave a talk on the composition of an orchestra, also on the different instruments. Major Orr, the eye specialist, left his patients or perhaps his afternoon nap, to give us a demonstration on his flute. His mastery of the latter instrument has lately earned him a seat in the AIF Orchestra, no small honour in itself, whilst from there his pipings may even reach Australia if the rumour we are hearing is correct: namely, that the Nipponese have decided to make a recording of our concert performance and to broadcast the same as an indication to the world of how happy we all are here at Selarang Barracks. I might add that, in today's demonstration, Major Orr seemed a little keyed up himself, and once or twice he grew red in the face and swore at his flute (gentlemanly swears) when it happened to emit a note an octave higher than the one intended, a habit which I have noticed is not uncommon with this instrument.

Wednesday, 8 September
On Wednesdays and Sundays there is no Japanese evening parade, which must be a relief to the Japanese.

Austin Edwards, our guest, arrived bronzed of face and well-groomed as always, wearing his smart safari jacket. On guest nights wine glasses are always put out and we toast the King, a custom which I always enjoy, although it is better when there is wine! (We use chlorinated water!)

Thursday, 9 September
Many of the men are suffering from amoebic dysentery.

Saturday, 11 September
Still rumoured that some bags of mail are at the Gaol and are being sorted. The latest dates are November 1942, (later A.G. MacAlister received one dated February 1943 from his wife in Brisbane) but I still live in hope of receiving some from home.

At the moment I am reading Gray Steel's *Life of General Smuts*, a prejudiced book but very interesting. The author tries to belittle his character but does not succeed because of the recorded facts. It is easy to vilify the great, but only if the truth is distorted. The writing of history sets a limit to this.

This afternoon I called to see Captain de Mowbray at present in the British Officers ward of building 175. He is very cheery, although pale and has swollen ankles. He was admitted for D and R, which he was relieved to find signified diet and rest — not death and ressurection!

At 7 p.m. I helped Carl Furner put his ducks away, then went to a hockey match. Later, with platform and lights specially arranged, the orchestra played in the Square.

Period to the End of September 1943
During this period two batches of prisoners came and went. They came from Java and went away again somewhere on ships after a brief stay in the hut encampment that we can see from here but which is cut off from us by the Changi-Singapore Road and by fences of barbed wire on each side thereof.

In the first party of about 500, some were British but the majority were Dutch of all shades of colour. A few from here obtained permission, to go and see them. The second party were about 2,000 strong, a few European Dutch but mostly coloured Dutch. There were two Dutch generals in this party, and about 30 Australians. I obtained permission with Frank Wright to go over and see them one afternoon. We sat in one of the huts and obtained news from a couple of young Indian Army officers.

End of September
There was news of more mail bags at the Gaol and everybody's spirits rose, at least I suppose they felt as I did. The lack of news leaves a hungry, aching void in one's life here with occasional pangs of anxiety. Sergeant David Griffin and Tony Newsom who had been sent to the gaol as mail sorters kindly sent me word that there was a postcard for me and, a few days later, a letter.

After the sorting, one still had to wait for the Japanese censors to finish before our mail arrived over here.

I waited for days for the prospect of news of all those at home. There was disappointment when it gradually became apparent that this was not fresh mail, but only leftover bags from the mail that arrived last March, seven months ago. All the letters received bore dates of July, August to December 1942.

1 October
Captain Bob Puflett returned from Blackangmati today with about 20 men, some sick, some returning here for a change after 18 months of work in Singapore. He was one of the two medical officers there. The other was Horace Tucker who is now alone but shortly to be joined by Captain Frankland of BGH. Puflett is an old boy from North Shore Grammar School. His experiences at Woodlands POW camp and Blackangmati Island, of which he gave a talk one day to officers here, were very interesting.

During October, there is not much to record
One afternoon the Japanese made a recording of one of the programs given by the AIF concert party. A couple of officers, including myself, and about 50 men from the hospital, went down to the theatre hall as part of a fairly large audience. The latter were asked to applaud as directed to enhance the effect. There was a microphone on the stage behind which, in a row, sat the members of the troupe. Captain Alan Bush did the announcing in mellifluous tones. The performers rose in turn and sang or spoke into the microphone. The officials present were a couple of Japanese officers and four or five technicians. Altogether, the performance took about two hours.

On Saturday nights I go to the serious music gramophone recitals on the lawn at the Convalescent Depot, and on Tuesday nights I play contract bridge with Frank Wright, Darrell Proctor (dentist of Mosman, Sydney) and Carl Furner; one week they come here and the following week Carl and I go over to their room at the Convalescent Depot. We also have the occasional talk in our own Officers Mess. Lieutenant-Colonel Middleton (BGH) gave a talk on Scotland (he commanded an ambulance in France). On another occasion, Padre Major Sandy from China gave a talk on medical education there. I arranged this talk as I wanted my medical officers to know something about the subject. After the war I hope there will be some liaison between our universities and the medical schools of China.

To go back a bit to 2 October, I formed a syndicate with Frank Wright and A.G. MacAlister of Southport and we purchased 18 baby ducks at 16 cents a head from the canteen. It was hard work finding or 'scrounging' material to build a yard and a duck house. We solved the latter with one of the steel cupboards used by a Gordon Highlander to put his clothes in when the Gordon's inhabited these barracks. There was much work, also, in rearing our babies during the first few weeks. Every time it rained, one had to dash out and race down four flights of stairs to save them from getting wet. Three died, but the other fifteen look well on the road to maturity.

On 29 October, George McNeilly (YMCA) gave a large party in their hut for Ivor Hangar's birthday. Colonel Galleghan was there. There were no speeches, just musical items. We devoured some very good imitation coconut lamingtons.

Monday, 1 November
All Saints' Day. I went to early church at St Luke's Chapel with my friend, our Chaplain Paine of Ballarat.

On Monday evenings, Captain de Gray gives his history lectures on the early history of Britain in the same Chapel.

It seems to rain every day and will continue like this until Christmas. The sun is rising further south as the winter begins.

I have heard the night bird, known as the 'clock bird', 'talking' in the distance, but only occasionally, so I suppose they are not all back yet to wherever they migrate.

Friday, 5 November
Fifty British and 50 Australians left today for Blackangmati; also Captain Frankland of BGH and Major Harold Park, dentist from our side. The men went cheerfully enough, poor fellows. They said the quarters were good there, the work loading bombs not too arduous, and the food passable, but there is the uncertainty as to their length of stay.

Sunday, 7 November
A football match between 197 Field Ambulance versus The Rest was played on the padang in aid of the Christmas Fund for the children in the Gaol. Collection boxes were taken around.

Monday, 8 November
I went over to the garden group with Bob Darby on a special invitation

from Scott Russell to share a cake. The latter had been made by their cook and was a good imitation of a seed cake.

In the evening I went to see the farce *Lord Baba* in the open-air theatre — very amusing.

Tuesday, 9 November
The letters received by English troops last month have been summarised as to news and the latter was read out to us by Benjamin, one of our padres. Some of the news was about Formosa where our first party of imprisoned senior officers was sent. There were several deaths from an epidemic there (probably diphtheria), and from intestinal worm infestation.

Mr Howl, late Attorney-General of Malaya, was reported to have died in Formosa. We were very sorry to hear of this, as he and Mrs Howl were very hospitable to Australians in 1941. I did not meet Mrs Howl but he came out and chatted for a while. Their daughter is married to an Australian RAF officer and is in Australia, fortunately not here.

Wednesday, 10 November
Alec Ogilvey came to dinner. Always a charming guest. The troupe have just finished *Outward Bound* in which he took the part of the examiner. The play was produced by Major Daltry, a difficult play to produce successfully before troops, but in spite of that it was most successful. Bradshaw and Daltry are both professional actors, Daltry lost an eye and a leg, (high amputation) and has to get around on crutches. Bradshaw, young and handsome, has been in Hollywood, I believe.

Thursday, 11 November — Armistice Day
At 10.45 a.m. went to C of E Chapel where prayers were held over the 11th hour period. The two-minute silence was observed throughout the POW area. I gave a few words to the men in my ward.

Sunday, 14 November
A Remembrance Day service was held in the Square in the evening with orchestra and choir. The latter, conducted by Glyn Williams, looked a bit ragged but sang well.

Recently a man escaped or disappeared from the POW area. He was one of those sent to hospital from Outram Rd Gaol on account of sickness. As a result, on Japanese orders, all other prisoners from the Singapore Gaol at Outram Road, who are now in hospital, have to be segregated.

I now have three officers and about ten other ranks from the AIF in my ground-floor ward. But three men were taken back to Outram Road Gaol, walking cheerfully across the square to join the Tommies from BGH.

Friday, 10 December
In the afternoon I made a toy boat for the children at the Gaol. Colonel

Julian Taylor, the London surgeon, is also making a toy boat, a large one. I don't know where he obtained his piece of wood — it looks like the leg of a billiard table. It is hard to get wood of any kind these days.

Monday, 13 December
I handed in my boat to Major Horton at Malaya Command who is painting the Christmas toys for the children in the Gaol.

An ambulance arrived from Singapore with the body of a Private Sims who had died in Singapore. It was reported that he had been up north.

Tuesday, 14 December
In the afternoon walked with Bill Bye to Divisional Headquarters, and saw the list of names of the first party who are now in Singapore and who may eventually come back here again; we don't know.

Wednesday, 15 December
Bad news has reached us from the north. F and H Forces which left here last April and May have suffered severely, out of a party of about 700 it is reported that over 200 are dead from cholera. From other places 900 British and other forces have died; we do not know if this includes Dutch.

Major Robertson of the 2nd Gurkhas came up at 11 a.m. and had a chat over a cup of tea. He brought the sad news that Digby Gates — the young Gurkha officer who had produced plays here last year — had died. (I saw him act in *Androcles and the Lion*.)

Thursday, 16 December
We have heard that some of our prisoners from overseas have arrived in the hut camp across the road, but we are not allowed to contact them. It was reported that 500 are to come into hospital (later 70 came).

Eight American airmen have recently been sent here. They are the survivors of the crews of four Liberators shot down in Indo-China, only eight out of 40 men. We understand that they have come from Hanoi.

This afternoon I attended a lecture on the heart by Carl Furner. The lecture ended early because of the arrival of the 70 sick troops from up-country: the forerunners of many to follow, as parties are to arrive here by train each night for several nights. The top floor of one building has been cleared for them.

In company with Carl Furner, Lieutenant Colonel Bye and Cotter Harvey and Captain Bob Puflett, I went to attend the newly arrived sick.

The new arrivals came across the road on trailers, many too weak to walk; however, most walked up the stairs to the ward just as we were arriving. They looked a sorry sight, lean, emaciated, gaunt, most affected by scabies and tinea and many had inflamed ulcers under dirty bandages, undressed for many days. Their unshaven pallor reminded me of 25 years ago, of exhausted men coming from the trenches after a battle.

The next two hours were busy ones. In between giving them attention, one gathered scraps of news: and the fate of F and H Forces, whose fate all these months had been shrouded in mystery, has begun to take shape in grim outlines drawn by our hospital orderlies who have returned.

I contacted Garett, one of our 13th AGH cooks, once fat and robust, now a shadow of his former self, also Corporal Chapman of the 10th AGH, and was saddened to learn of the death of young Sweetman, something personal to me as we had begun the war together at General Base Camp at Johore Bahru.

The party across the road is Colonel Kappe's force and they have come down by steamer from near Bangkok and also by train. There are officers in F Force including Colin Juttner who is sick. I went to the Officers ward later to see him and to hear his tragic story of the march: 196 miles through a jungle track — much hardship, midges, mud, dysentery, calamitous sickness, lack of shelter, constant rain, climbs up steep slippery hillsides often in deep mud.

Major Bruce Hunt's name stands out amongst those many medical officers whose names are spoken of in terms of admiration and gratitude by the men. Men and officers have returned devoid of personal belongings, even, almost, of clothing.

1944

Wednesday, 19 January
In the early morning I sat in the sunshine at the wide open sliding window of the small house No. 214: below in the garden frangipani, yellow cassia, gardenia shrubs in flower and the red flowering bush. Beyond is a wide green vista, palms, casuarinas and a glimpse of the waters of the Straits. It is a relief to be away from the noisy Barrack and the sad sights of the hospital.

I have been here 12 days, attached now to Major Bosley's B Group, detachments of those gunners and engineers who did not go up country. Sharing these pleasant quarters with Major Bosley are also Lieutenant Graham of Grafton and Captain Kinder ex-Malay Police Force.

There are numerous little yellow butterflies amongst the shrubs in the garden below and a 'flame of the forest' (poinciana tree), not in flower at present but laden with its long black bean pods. Ducks and cows wander on the lawn and, amongst them, the ubiquitous Indian myna bird — a kind of yellow-billed starling. On the tiled roof, the sparrows chirp happily.

These houses, built for families of the Garrison troops, are well constructed and in good repair, except those few spattered by the bombs of February 1942. Most of them bear the date of 1937 or 1938 on their facades, and in those years this area, which is the healthiest and most picturesque on Singapore Island, was thrown open to the Garrison troops. The general feeling now is that those troops then settled down to a comfortable life, and neglected to train for the hardships and intricate manoeuvres of jungle warfare on the Peninsula.

In the palm grove beyond our garden, there are two long atap huts and a couple of small marquee tents where live some of my erstwhile friends of C Group and their officers, Bill Jones of Casino and Don Garner of Sydney amongst them.

Two hundred yards to the south of this house, and just across the bitumen main road, Changi to Singapore, is the area where the large collection of huts on or around the padang at present provide a home for those AIF members of F Force who are now back here after their eight months up country where they took part in the construction of the infamous railway. All the AIF of F Force are back except such as are still in hospital, too sick for the four and a half days train journey.

Only a portion of British F Force seems to be back. I saw young Wycherley, the pianist and accompanist, but all the rest of the celebrity concert party, who used to entertain us so delightfully both here and at Roberts Barracks have been wiped out by disease, with the exception of the violinist Denis East. The latter, we hear, is still in hospital up north, but recovering. Padre Foster Haig, the singer and leader, has died, also my friend, George Wall (gunner), the baritone. East will miss him as they were friends and studied together at the London College of Music. Also, Renison, the pianist, has died.

Soon after the parties arrived up there last April and May, dysentery struck them, then cholera. In spite of the inoculation, one injection per man, which was given before they left here. All developed malaria, almost without exception, and many developed beri-beri.

Since the last date of entry, I have taken part in some hard work at the hospital and seen much tragedy and death from sickness. The men are so emaciated from malaria and other diseases that they die easily. I shared the work of a ward that occupied the whole top floor of a Barrack Square building, the patients numbering 45-50. Major Ian Cameron attended to the rest. We had over 100 patients all told and worked together from 20 December to 7 January. On this latter date, Major Clive Uhr developed acute appendicitis and was sent to hospital from here for an operation. I was sent across to take his place and do his work, hence my being here.

I was sorry to hand over my patients at the hospital but, at the same time, it came as a rest from the hard work and I had been unwell from a recurring sore throat and several sleepless nights from the irritating cough that followed. I was sorry, also, to leave my dormitory neighbours and pals at the hospital — Carl Furner and Bob Puflett. I don't know officially whether I am here permanently or only as a locum tenens. One is not told these things by our Hospital Commander and I do not ask for the reason that I do not want it to be thought that I am asking for any consideration.

In my opinion the glamour and privilege that attach to army rank are more in evidence in the AIF than in the BEF here in Changi, so much so that one sometimes wonders whether it is entirely forgotten that we are just as much prisoners of war awaiting an uncertain fate and, fundamentally, we are all in the same bag.

The conditions in the wards of the hospital have reminded me, in many ways, of the early days at Roberts Barracks in March and April 1942, when dysentery hit us and when the severely wounded men were at the height of their suffering and death rate. Now, as then, there is confusion, overwork, shortage of material, stoppage of the water supply lasting several days, and nights of complete darkness owing to blackouts. This time, moreover, there are no supplies available from Red Cross stores.

As regards news of friends who have been absent, I have seen Jim Crombie several times, a shadow of his former self, but picking up slowly. I went to see him across the road as soon as the quarantine ban had been lifted. Whilst there, I also visited Corporal Rob Salway of Southport, and Vincent O'Reilly from Upper Coomera, Captain Brian Ferguson and Padre Pollaine, also of the 2/26th Battalion, and Lieutenant Uroe. Sad to relate, Sid Bignell died up-country, now the second of that family in the Upper Coomera whom this war has claimed. I remember enlisting him into the militia at Southport before the war. Also, it has been reported that poor Dave Gallagher of Southport has died. Many of H Force, AIF, are in Singapore at Syme Road, but we are not in contact with them. I have heard Dick Pockley is there and fairly well, thank goodness. As regards our old 13th AGH members, I have no news of dear old Geoff Davies our pathologist, nor of Tim Hogg of Launceston. We heard that they had been sent by the Japanese to look after the medical care of native labour gangs.

As regards Christmas and New Year festivities, these were curtailed and dimmed by the return of the up-country men and their admittance to hospital. However, we did have a Christmas dinner at the AGH and it included roast pork, a small succulent slice each; very nice. Also, a bottle of whisky was presented by Major Harry Phillips, the Mess President, who had kept it all this time since the capitulation. It is possible that our gratitude for the gift, which was enormous, equalled our admiration for him for his months of self-restraint! Anyway, it gave each of the 30 of us a small port glass of whisky in which to drink the health of His Majesty. The Nipponese Supervising Officer presented each individual with a Christmas gift of a packet of 20 cigarettes which was very acceptable.

The convalescent officer patients at the Convalescent Depot, under the catering of Corporal Rose, Private Faunt of Enniskillen Station, Queensland, and Lieutenant Swaddling, Mess Secretary, gave a party on Christmas morning to which I was invited. Gordon Stronach and other Queenslanders were there, altogether about 40 to 50 officers. It was a very happy and cheerful gathering and the various doovers and slices were quite exceptional. Instead of cocktails, we had black coffee.

There have been two Christmas pantomimes, *Aladdin* at the little theatre, the former building where Smokey Joe's restaurant used to be. The walls of the big entertainment hall still carry the cartoons in black and white, painted by Private Rogan of the Convalescent Depot, depicting Walt Disney figures and similar characters. This hall, being in the original NAAFI building, had a proper stage and they have enhanced the effect by rooting up the floor in front of the stage and constructing a pit for the orchestra. The building is used by BGH medical officers as sleeping and eating quarters upstairs. The theatrical troupe holds sway on the ground floor.

Aladdin was a great hit; plenty of fun in the old pantomime style. Padre Wearne, with his good singing voice, was very successful as the Chinese Emperor, whilst Hugh Elliot, as Widow Twankey, was the perfect pantomime dame. Backshall as Aladdin gave a good representation of the principal boy in doublet tights and short gumboots. We managed to wheel John Wyett and Mac in chairs down to see *Aladdin* and they thoroughly enjoyed it.

The other pantomime at the AIF theatre was also excellent: the stage scenery was by Murray Griffin, the war artist, and the libretto was by Leslie Greener the novelist.

On Christmas morning I went to early Communion at St Luke's Chapel. Padre Chambers officiated. Not many were present, but I believe many attended the midnight service by Padre Pain. It was quite dark at the beginning of our service, but there is an electric bulb in the Chapel. The early morning silence was only broken by the Padre's gentle voice and the singing of the little black and white robin known in Malaya as a magpie, the sweetest song bird I have ever heard here or, indeed, almost anywhere, rivalling our golden whistler.

During the busy time in December, the care of our 16 ducks became a burden at times, and only the unremitting care of A.G. MacAlister kept it going. We raised 14 out of our original 18, bought at one-day-old last 1 October. The two other adults now laying were acquired by arrangement.

When I came to B Group, old Mac and Frank Wright got orders to move the ducks to the Convalescent Depot. They moved their share after some little trouble, leaving the others as the share belonging to me and Fred Finch. The order they received from Colonel Webster and Colonel Summons was to move the ducks the same day. It could not be done, nor was there any reason for such an order. With the lack of material for making yards, it is no easy matter these days to provide accommodation for poultry. Ducks are easier than hens to handle because of the high fences needed for the latter. I have spent several afternoons constructing a fence round my spinach patch at the duck yard. I made it out of the stems of palm fronds stripped of leaves and fixed together by strands of barbed wire.

I was interested in the question of a sufficient supply of eggs for the emaciated and sick men at the hospital. Voluntary giving seemed, to me, to have failed. Some gave freely but others moaned and gave miserably, regarding the eggs as their rightful property, earned by months of hard work. This was quite true up to a point. I know from experience it is hard work to rear ducks under the conditions pertaining here, but we have to remember that our fellow soldiers, who have been building the railway 600 miles up north, have not had the chance to 'work hard' in the duck yards of Changi in order to produce eggs for themselves in due season. They had been working hard at something else, under conditions beyond and outside anything that we fortunate ones, who had been left behind, had ever experienced.

Personally, I was so worried by the difficulty of obtaining eggs for the emaciated patients that I wrote to Lieutenant-Colonel Glyn White, the ADMS, expressing my feelings on this subject of commandeering eggs for the patients, and I am sure he felt as I did. A copy of my letter follows.

After consultations at Headquarters, it has been decided to buy as many eggs as the hospital requires — 25 cents for duck eggs and 20 cents for hen eggs. This is more than I would personally have voted to poultry owners, but on the other hand, if the money is at hand it might as well be used. The main thing is to get the eggs, and canteen eggs are now up to 45 cents when obtainable, and far from fresh at that.

Selarang Changi,
January 1944

Dear Glyn,

I hope you will forgive me for writing unofficially, i.e. as a doctor other than as a medical officer. It is on the subject of the up-country patients now in hospital.

For three weeks prior to my coming here to B Group (I was sent to relieve the MO who went to hospital with appendicitis), I helped Ian Cameron look after one of the wards with 125-130 patients. When they first came in the middle of December from the north, where nearly half had died under the Japanese engineers building the Bangkok/Moulmein Railway, I thought the cases not so bad as they all walked up the stairs. However, it gradually dawned on me how weak and how riddled with malaria these men were. The first week we had in our ward two deaths, the second another two, the third week one death I think, and now, today, two more have died in that ward. Relapses of malaria and persistent diarrhoea — the latter I think partly due to the bean diet which we are obliged to give them — are keeping numbers of them in a precarious state. In fact, it seems to me that we shall continue to lose a good many and that we are facing a crisis somewhat similar to February, March and April 1942, when dysentery emaciation and suppurating war wounds were accompanied by an inadequate diet.

About early April 1942 I told Colonel Pigdon that there were about 25 to 30 men in the hospital, apart from those acutely ill, who seemed to me likely to go gradually down hill unless they had special attention and special feeding. I suggested that the padres and the Red Cross personnel form a team to attend and feed them. Colonel Pigdon asked me for a list of names which I gave him. A much better scheme was then formulated by Colonel Pigdon, possibly after consultation with yourself and Colonel Durham, whereby these cases of malnutrition were all brigaded together in the Sergeants Mess ward. My original 30 were sent there plus about as many more selected by the MOs in charge of wards. There is no doubt the system saved some lives.

In the present crisis we have not, of course, the same supplies in the Red Cross store as we had then; nevertheless, there are, I understand, some hundreds of tins of fish being held in reserve. Also, there are many hundreds of eggs now being produced daily in the POW area which are being consumed by people who are not sick. In my recent ward at the Australian hospital, our daily egg ration was between 10 and 16 eggs amongst 125 men in the ward, so that, in my opinion, the voluntary system of giving eggs has failed. Some give and some do not give.

An officer for collecting and distributing eggs (Captain Finch) has been appointed at the AGH and this is a good precedent for each group to adopt.

I have two suggestions to meet this sickness and starvation crisis and, if you think them worthwhile, I hope you will pass them on to the British ADMS and the Administration Headquarters of both British and AIF:

1. That all eggs be commandeered during the present crisis for hospital, if necessary at a fixed price of, say, 10 cents;

2. That all patients that are dangerously emaciated be grouped into one ward or half a ward for special attention and special dieting, as far as the latter is possible, by the adoption of such measures as are embodied in the first suggestion.

Yours...........

(Sgd) Charles Huxtable

January 1944
I am enjoying my work at B Group. In my department I have Corporal Parnell of Albany, W.A., Corporal Lister, and Private Winters. I have

a sick parade morning and evening, 450 men in the group. About half have to be supplied daily for work at ground levelling and a certain number for work in the big gardens. The group contains the remainder of the engineers and gunners who did not go up north, also a few special groups, base supply depot workers, canteen workers, etc. Most are Class 3 men i.e. unfit for the north.

The broom factory for the AIF is situated on our ground floor and is in the capable hands of Corporal Roche, who was Manager of Dondaroo Station, near Winton, Qld, and knows Jim Crombie, also the Cobbs and others from the area. A group with Alan McLean and Jock White are only a hundred yards down the road, so I often see them and I sometimes see Bob Skene and Forestry fellows and the Indian Army Officers Mess where my chief acquaintance is Major Robertson.

Friday, 5 February

Recently I had an opportunity to send a note into Syme Road, Singapore, to Dick Pockley and can only hope it reaches him.

A couple of weeks ago we heard there were nearly 3,000 letters at the Gaol for the AIF — nearly one each. More recently, one of our men, who has been sorting, told me he had seen one for me. It is from England; I hope with news from home, and I am still hoping for another from home. Great patience is required, waiting for the wearisome censoring to be done. It is reported that there are 1,639 letters for AIF soldiers who are dead or missing. It is sad to think about all that wasted love and anxiety put into the penning of those letters and of the enclosures — many will contain family photographs — now all to waste their sweetness on the desert air.

Yesterday Gunner Bagot of the 2/15 Field Regiment died suddenly — a heart attack. There had been no previous heart attack although he was an older man, i.e. he looked 60, although his Army age was only 52. It was an easy way for an old soldier of the last war. He did indeed just 'fade away', but after surviving two years as a POW it seems hard luck.

After a two-hour hunt through the wood heap this morning, one of the men extracted a black cobra — 3'10" long.

Saturday, 6 February

This afternoon Gunner Bagot's funeral was held. I am told that there were over 100 of the Regiment there under Lieutenant-Colonel Wright.

Sunday, 7 February

I walked across in the early dawn to Holy Communion at St Luke's Chapel near the Hospital, calling in by arrangement to pick up John Wyett; he cannot walk yet but gets about with the aid of a wheelchair, a very battered chair and the only one in the possession of the Australian Hospital. Padre Jones officiated.

After getting John back to his bed, I was a bit late returning for breakfast at 9 a.m. and sick parade at 9.30. The men who work at ground levelling on the aerodrome go daily to work, except on Fridays which is a rest day for them (Sunday is a working day).

Monday, 8 February
Some letters from home were delivered this evening. Most people got one or two. I had none from home. It is now nearly a year since I had letters from home and no news later than August 1942, nearly 18 months ago. The latest dated letters of which I have heard were written August 1943. Major Robertson and others have letters from India — India and South Africa seem to be in much closer touch with this area. I did have one letter from England, dated 1 January 1943.

Wednesday, 10 February
In the evening I went to the little theatre with Major Bosley to see Noel Coward's *Hay Fever*, witty and amusing. Major Daltry, overcoming all difficulties, produced a first-class show and the acting was very good. John Wood, the Australian, was Mrs Bliss and Major Bradshaw her husband. We had a good laugh and all agreed that we had often paid ten bob to see shows of a far lower standard in peace time.

Today, by the way, I saw young Wycherley of the former celebrity artists. He and Denis East are the sole survivors and the latter still in hospital up north. I hope he gets back here.

Saturday, 13 February
The Japanese have ordered each of us to write a short account of some anecdote or adventure that each has experienced during the war in Malaya.

For lunch today I went to the Convalescent Depot to join MacAlister, Frank and Fred Finch for a poultry stew — the first of our poultry. Mac was the caterer and an excellent one. Two drakes went west yesterday. We each gave in 25 cents and procured sweet potatoes and bananas with the total sum, and all of it went to make up an excellent pot.

Sunday, 14 February
Back to duty at the hospital — to the top floor of the same old three-storey building in the Barrack Square. I regretted leaving the good medical team behind. 'Sailor' Eldridge welcomed me back and fixed my bed inside; the balcony had so much glare that it gave me headaches, so I decided to abandon Carl Furner and place my bed between George Brady and Lindsay Orr. I'm to work on the top floor of the building opposite, a medical ward with the usual 120-140 patients.

Period February 15 to Anzac Day
Admissions of malaria cases keep us busy, most of them relapses among those who have come from the north and almost all benign tertian. But

a fairly high proportion, too high for comfort, are coming from primary malaria contracted here at Changi. It appears that our anti-malaria squads recently have not been able to work on the new aerodrome being constructed, hence an increase in anopheles breeding; the latter supposed to be chiefly *sundiacus* breeding in salt-water swamps or that neighbourhood. Whilst I was with B Group (5 weeks) I had about 25 cases of primary infection. The men working at ground-levelling on the 'drome get very tired, long hours from 8.30 a.m. start and after 6.00 p.m. arriving back at camp.

Our diet in March altered again, rice was cut down and maize substituted. At breakfast, we each had a plate of crushed maize. Also, there are no potatoes (we used to have sweet potatoes) these days, the crops in the gardens seem to grow leaves but no spuds. We have fallen back on tapioca which is not bad fried in bits like potato chips. Also tapioca flour makes very good pastry. Our cooks excel at it, especially out Officers' cook, Bill Nelson, the Scot. There is no more fish — not greatly missed because it is usually so small, bony and hard to eat — although one does miss very much the occasional steaks of shark or stingray which made excellent eating. We now get fresh meat occasionally, 'yak' as it is called; probably the humped Indian cattle brought from the north or from Saigon. Anyway, it is very acceptable, even though rare, and only about four pieces each one cubic inch in size. Later, when General Saito took over in March, we got meat a little more frequently, every two to three days.* For midday, we have doovers, i.e. fried rissoles made from tapioca or rice flour generally flavoured (and how little is required to give a flavour) with dried fish of the kind used by the Chinese. Very dry and very high! Also a couple of tablespoons of rice and some black daizu beans. For dinner at night we have a cup of bean and rice soup, rather watery as a rule unless a meat night, doovers or meat pasties, some rice and soya beans, a dessertspoon of green spinach, then a sweet consisting of a piece of pastry and some ground rice sauce, often flavoured with coffee, very nice, remnants of the Red Cross parcels. The latter were a gift from Uncle Sam, a Godsend while they lasted. (The Japanese retained hundreds of these parcels.)

There are only a few Americans in camp, one naval officer, six flying officers and a couple of dozen men. These few donated the Red Cross parcels to the whole camp: parcels, well packed, chiefly tins. As personal perquisites, each of us got one packet of cigarettes (20), one piece of chocolate about as big as a man's thumb, and a small square of soap, about two cubic inches. The latter is good for shaving and my piece has lasted for weeks. For the Mess we received tinned cheese, bacon and eggs in the tin, and coffee essence, the two former just enough to provide a small helping each for one meal, not much but a welcome break. The coffee essence has been most useful as a flavouring agent.

*Until then the POWs were considered 'captives'. Now the Japanese recognised them as Prisoners of War and sometimes observed parts of the Geneva Convention.

On Wednesday afternoon, General Saito addressed a large parade of all British and Australian troops in the Barrack Square. The Medical Officers had to be on duty in their wards and were not allowed to look down. The General mounted an improvised platform at one end of the Square and gave his address — short and to the point. He said: 'I am Saito. I have taken over command of the POW camp. I will make no change. You will obey orders and regulations of the Imperial Nipponese Army. If I see the necessity for changes, I will make them.' This was translated for us by a Japanese interpreter who stood beside the General.

At a birthday of Ian McLean's on 17 March I met a one-legged Englishman; a fine-looking man in his 30s, who has lost a fine limb if one can judge by its fellow left behind. Like Alan McLean's loss, it is above the knee, so he goes on crutches. His name is Hugo Hughes of the Malayan Regiment and he was seriously wounded in fighting on Singapore Island towards the last few days. (He had been a planter here and obtained a commission in the Malayan Regiment.) We had not been talking long when I discovered he comes from Edinburgh and is a brother of Mrs Denham of Southport. A few days later, he came to afternoon tea with me here. That was in the latter good days when we could afford some hospitality, such as mashed banana, to a guest! Now there are no bananas at the canteen to buy and very little else. By the end of April prices had risen to absurd levels, and apart from prices, very little comes in. Sugar rose to $3.60 per lb. and gula malacca to $2.75, coconuts 80 cents each, cigars 13 cents each. Thanks to a generous cash gift sent me by Dick Pockley from Syme Road, I bought a supply of gula malacca and peanuts $2.20 a lb. The former I used to sweeten the morning porridge, the latter roasted by the cook for me, and I occasionally take a handful.

In the middle of March a new disease arrived to trouble us, raw and ulcerated lips, mouth and, in bad cases, throats. Three of the latter have died and have been found to have lung lesions. Many are showing a severe rash — path tests have shown a pellagrous infection of the mucous membranes of the mouth and throat. Lieutenant-Colonel Wright of the 13th Field Regiment, AIF, is in the Officers ward suffering severely.

Fortunately, the malaria is easing off. I lost a man, Private Young, 2/26th Battalion from Brisbane who died from acute nephritis with oedema. Another Brisbane lad from up north named Galvin died of a curious lung condition which proved to be cancer. Another, named Curtis from Ravenshoe, died from ulceration of the lower part of the ilium with symptoms of obstruction of the bowel.

We get occasional news from H Party at Syme Road Camp in Singapore. Roy Mills, a young Medical Officer who has been up north, came in from there sick but has now joined our staff here. He belonged originally to the 10th Field Ambulance. I have had notes from both Dick Pockley and Laurie West and I have written to them and sent Dick a pair of trousers (he was always short of trousers) and a couple of books.

There has also been news from there of Russell Braddon, Peter Playfair and the Davis brothers, friends of Dick.

In March and April, Lieutenant Colonel Bill Bye lectured twice weekly on neurology. As usual, these were excellent.

Jock Douglas from Syme Road and Bill Brooker (from Springbrook, Qld) are in a ward in the next block. I often see them and occasionally obtain books for them — books are one of the great needs nowadays. Lester Brooker, who is thin and ill, has been sent as unfit with a party that went to Syme Road. From time to time I see cheerful, red-faced Sam Moffitt from Mudgeeraba to remind me of the rural scenes of home.

We have many good theatrical shows:

The AIF troupe performs in the big theatre which is the relic of a large engineering building with iron girders and iron roof, completely open on the north side. It has a stage and bench seats and an overhead platform for spotlights, a pit for the orchestra, a fenced-in area below the stage. The shows are always bright and amusing, if somewhat lowbrow — clever singing, dancing, female impersonation (John Woods) and conjuring tricks (Sid Piddington).

Then there is the Phoenix Theatre over near the Malaya Command building, half a mile away, over by No. 3 gate. It is an open-air theatre and the two active participants are a young officer named Fitzgerald and Major Sheehan of Malaya Command. Here we saw Wodehouse's *Good Morning, Bill,* also Edgar Wallace's *On the Spot,* and again, a clever and moving play, *Love on the Dole.* The actors in the latter were mainly private soldiers and NCOs (British). The scene is the slums of Lancashire and the three old women were superb — accent and acting perfect — the heroine, Sally, although too tall for the hero, was not unattractive. One night we went to this little theatre with John Wyett and young MacAlister to see the play *Suspect,* very good drama indeed. A young Lieutenant, John White (British Army) was one of the female impersonators: a few weeks later his sore lips and mouth extended suddenly to the throat and he died within a few days.

17 March
I asked Lieutenant-Colonel Glyn White to interview Private Jim Crombie of the 29th Battalion who is not at all well. In his usual sympathetic way, Glyn White took the case up and had Jim sent into this hospital today, a shadow of his former self — 6'5" and only 9 stone in weight.

Easter Sunday, 9 April
I went to the Communion Service early to-day with Bill Barnes at St Luke's Chapel. This little square Chapel with its red-tiled roof was soon afterwards taken over as a sleeping place for troops when the rest of F Force came down from Thailand. Services then had to be held in various parts of the hospital buildings or in outbuildings, Mess huts, etc.

Sunday, 16 April
Lieutenant-Colonel Holmes of the Manchester Regiment addressed all officers on matters of reorganisation and discipline. The AIF theatre was packed — a very good address, authoritative but polite as from one gentleman to others.

Sunday, 23 April
Anzac Day Services were held in the different churches.

After lunch I went with Carl Furner and Bob Puflett to the prison area across the road, and there we joined up with Captain Shute and some others from his group and a party led by Group Captain Hank Moore from this side. We marched to the beach, about a mile, under an escort of three Japanese soldiers and had a half hour swim in the sea, still water and rather a muddy bottom, but still a treat. The Japanese swam, too; they were kindly disposed and brought us back in an empty lorry — two journeys to fetch the lot of us, which saved us the long hot walk under the coconut palms.

Tuesday, 25 April
I attended an open air dawn service taken by Padres Jones and Benjamin on the slope of the hill beyond the old Convalescent Depot; about 50 were present. Colonel Galleghan read the lines 'We will remember them'. The birds were singing with us as we gathered under the rubber trees.

We are killing off most of the ducks because of the lack of food. The hospital refuse (i.e. there are about 700 to 800 patients and staff in the AIF wing of the hospital at present) is now barely enough to feed 100 ducks. About 70 of these belong to men and sergeants of the staff and about 30 or more to the syndicates formed by officers. One day a small dog was boiled and cooked with the duck food, rather revolting, as it was very red meat.

I read and enjoyed C.B. Fry's *Life Worth Living* (the famous cricketer) and sent some books and a note to Dick Pockley on Syme Road who generously sent me out $20.

Shortly after Anzac Day, the troops from Syme Road (H party) began to send us their sick. Dick Pockley, Peter Playfair and many others who had been up-country with H Force still bore the effects. Dick had ulcers on the leg and Peter recurrent malaria.

Our cases are medical, most are malaria or swollen legs, beri-beri, some with emaciation and severe anaemia. During my few weeks work in the ward I lost a Brisbane lad with acute nephritis; another named Grosser almost died of an ulcerated mouth, high fever and a blood condition which appeared, at first, incurable — agranulo cytosis — a total white blood cell count of 200 per cmm. The hospital (AGH) still seems to lose one or two men a week. Young, who died in my dysentery ward last Christmas, used then to complain of bronchitis and pains in the chest. Coming down from Thailand on that shocking rail journey of five days, he lay sick with dysentery on the floor of the truck. At a stopping place it was given out that there was food on the platform so the troops scrambled to get out. They were mixed British and Australian. Galvin, a little underweight man, received a hard kick in the chest from some man who said 'If you don't want to get out yourself, get out of the bloody road'. He thought that his chest pains dated from that brutal kick, but it was not so because it was found after his death that he had a large malignant growth in the chest (mediastinum). Such a pity that despair and misery should have brutalised that man that gave the kick, just at the time when they were on the verge of receiving at least some relief and comfort from their sufferings.

I often saw my friend, John Wyett, surely one of the nicest of men, and his room-mate the cheery and gallant young Mac whose foot is still in plaster because of a fracture of a metatarsal bone. *

About the middle of May there came a bombshell — a big move is to take place and a splitting up of the POWs into two main groups. The larger group, roughly 8,000, is to be transferred from here to Changi Gaol. To accommodate them, the civilian internees including the women and children will move from the Gaol to Syme Road. The POWs at Syme Road will join the party going to the Gaol. The second and smaller group will go to some camp at present undetermined but probably many miles away, either at the other end of Singapore Island or in Johore. This latter group is to be pre-eminently a hospital group which will include all chronic and seriously ill patients.

Jim Crombie is in hospital at last, under the kind and skilful care of Captain Bob Puflett.

The rumours gradually crystalised into a more or less definite report that the new hospital would be at or near Kranji, about 20 miles away over near the Straits of Johore and close by the main road which leads from Singapore City to Johore Bahru. The staff will be combined British and Australian. The team of officers from our side was picked, about two weeks before we left, as follows: Lieutenant-Colonels Webster, Osborne, Cotter Harvey; Majors Harry Phillips, Carl Furner, and Roy Stevens; Captains Catchlove, Puflett, Conlon, Woodruff, Juttner, Hendry and myself. The Chaplains Aubrey Paine and Hugh Jones, and our old quartermaster, George Braby, as a patient.

Meantime, during May, the troops, not the hospital patients, began preparations to move into the Gaol. Each morning and afternoon large convoys of hand-pulled trailers were drawn up on the Barrack Square, loaded with all varieties of material, kitchen and building materials, large sections of demolished huts which had to be re-erected around the Gaol as there is only accommodation inside for about 3,000 to 4,000. The

---

* Mac had asked the author to break his leg so that he would be able to stay in hospital. Captain Huxtable refused to do this but agreed to fracture a metatarsal bone with a sledge-hammer as the only means of keeping him there.

rest will live outside in huts or out-buildings and will be surrounded, as here, by an enclosing barbed wire fence. Quite a strange sight to see a long string of man-pulled trailers stretching out along the road in an apparently endless procession. Officers as well as men compose the teams. The lucky, or perhaps disabled, member sat at the wheel of each trailer and worked wheel and brakes. Syme Road troops were the first to be moved into the Gaol, some for whom quarters were not yet ready came to Selarang including several of our former Medical Officers — Bruce Hunt, Kevin Fagan and Roy Mills. It was nice to see Kevin Fagan again, though very sick-looking at first from repeated malaria attacks. He and Bruce Hunt are the idols, amongst the Medical Officers, of the troops who were in the north.

I conceived the idea of looking over the Gaol as once our party leaves here for Kranji there will probably be no further chance for me to see it. So, one morning after finishing ward work, I took French leave and went to the hut area across the road where I knew Bernie Schult was dismantling huts. He arranged for me to have a lift in a truck and I sailed along the Singapore Road in fine style. The drive was all too short and, after turning left at the Gaol, I met one-armed Eric Boyd who took me into the main entrance past the Japanese guard.

This was the first time I had had a close-up view of the Gaol. For the past 18 months I have seen it from a distance and heard the clock chiming. I went up all floors. The cells are concrete and are very small, made for one man but now are to hold three — one to sleep on the concrete bed platform and two on the stone floor on either side of him. Many prefer to sleep in the corridor outside, even over the grid. On the walls of the cells were some writings of good cheer left by the civilian prisoners to greet the soldiers. One requested that the new inhabitants should be kind to Oscar the spider, 'whom we have looked after for two years'. Another cell was marked as Lady Shenton's cell (the Governor's wife).

The Gaol has a shut-in oppressive gloom about it. The winding iron stairways, long narrow corridors, the prison yards, spacious in parts but hemmed in by 30-foot walls, all combine to depress the spirits and to make one thankful for not having to come here; although we have heard reports that our future camp at Kranji is not the pleasantest. The huge Gaol kitchens, however, do provide some relief after the dingy makeshift, open-air affairs we have hitherto lived with. The clock booms out the hour. One wonders how the women and children are faring, having left here so recently for other quarters in Singapore.

On the way out I met Jack Smith, commedienne of the AIF concert party, in a corridor looking a bit lost. He is hoping to get a theatre going soon in one of the yards.

Passing out through the big gates, one salutes the Japanese guard sitting under the clock tower. Outside the gates, vegetable gardens extend down the hill in front. At the sides of the Gaol away from the main road, which skirts the northern flank, numerous hut buildings from Selarang (dragged across on trailers by manpower) are being erected to accommodate the 5,000-odd men and officers who are lucky enough to be going to live outside. There are to be about 3,000 inside. The whole outside area, of course, is enclosed by barbed wire.

Sunday, 31 December
A gap of seven long months has elapsed and now follows a brief summary of the leaving of Selarang Barracks and the hospital there, and the arrival at Woodlands Kranji Camp on 28 May 1944, where the subsidiary hospital is established under Lieutenant Colonel Collins, RAMC.

Kranji Camp is a hut encampment previously used as a hospital for sick Indian POWs and is situated at the 13½ mile stone on the main road, Bukit Timah Road, north of Singapore City, and 2½ miles on the south side of the Causeway leading across the Straits of Johore. From the Parade ground we can see part of Johore Bahru town across the Straits, including the great mosque, part of a sultan's palace and the big, modern, red-brick hospital where we doctors attended some interesting clinics before the fighting began. From the little hill beside the camp, where the cemetery is situated, one can see a lovely view including the fine square tower of the municipal buildings of Johore Bahru. Southwards the view is cut off by higher ground and one can only see trees and a couple of other hills when one looks towards Singapore and the south. The camp is more-or-less circular and placed in a rubber plantation, which is rather pleasant because of the shade thrown by the trees which grow in rows between the huts.

1945

The Beginning of the End — 21 July 1945
We have heard through our secret wireless equipment that the Australian 9th Division are doing well at Brunei Bay, North Borneo, with the 7th Division fighting around Balikpapan where they landed on 1 July. The Japanese have been beaten in Burma and we hope Australian troops will soon attack Eastern Borneo, Kuching or Natuna Island.

24 July
Allied planes are attacking the Japanese Navy in the inland sea, and our war ships are shelling the mainland.

27 July
We have heard that Mr Attlee has replaced Mr Churchill as Prime Minister of Britain and that Labour is in with a big majority. Padre Patten is much distressed. I confess I feel a little worried about the Labour Party being in power in England and so do most of the British Officers here.

Early in August the Japanese authorities closed our theatre, ordered the stage to be dismantled and advised us of a big move at or before the end of August. The term 'Japanese Authorities' is not correct — I should have written 'the Japanese Sergeant of the Guard of this Camp', an ignorant and vulgar coolie addicted to alcohol.

The loss of the theatre and of our entertainment concerts and plays is somewhat depressing. We are still allowed to use the big wooden hall on Sunday nights for Church Services but not for the evening lectures, all of which are now countermanded.

The move at the end of August is to be as follows:

All medical officers from here, except half a dozen, all patients and all medical personnel, are to move to Changi Gaol to join the major POW group there. All combatant officers, British and Australian, are to move from Changi to here. This is to be a POW Officers' Camp. Major Bradshaw and his command in the area adjoining this hospital area, some 1,000 in all, will stay on here as a working party as they are at present. Presumably they will go out each day into the surrounding countryside and dig dug-outs for the Japanese against the coming invasion. The medical officers who will stay here will form the staff of a small local hospital for any officers who may become sick. The officers who are sick at present in the two officers' huts will also presumably remain here. I am to return to Changi. I have mixed feelings about that, but from the point of view of safety in the event of the suspected invasion by our forces, Changi would appear to be a 'better 'ole' in the words of old Bill.

Carl Furner is one of those picked to stay here, which I deeply regret; sorry to part from him and sorry for the uncertainty of this place — which he realises and philosophically accepts. I am also deeply sorry that so many of my officer friends from Changi will be coming here.

The work continues in the 'wards'. In my hut (23), I have a dozen beri-beri cases of a severe type, bloated, anaemic and waterlogged. The food for the patients is wretched and most of such cases will die if present conditions continue. They cannot pick up on a rice diet of only 230 grammes (8¼ oz) a day, as well as ½ oz fish, dried 'whitebait' so called, and a few miserable vegetables in the form of spinach and potato tops. Most of the 'greens' available come from our gardens which adjoin the camp and are worked by our staff and convalescent patients. A small issue comes from Japanese rations. We continue to lose about two men a week. The diagnosis in recent cases has been indefinite, and sometimes includes the term 'inanition', a polite medical term for starvation. We have made free use of the vitamin tablets sent to us by the American Red Cross and handed over to us by the Japanese some three months ago; however, the results are disappointing. Better nutrition is needed, as well as vitamins. There is the feeling, too, that the vitamins have lost potency owing to the long delay in arrival.

A word now on human nature:

There are some in camp who are not only well but also fat. These include cooks and racketeers. Cooks are allowed extra food officially, and this is good policy for two reasons: firstly it leaves them no justification for taking more, and secondly, they have long hours and hard work and have to be kept healthy. But hangers-on at cook houses are an abomination and so are those who steal rations, rice, sugar or salt, either for their own eating or in order to sell. It is hard, if not impossible, to prove that the latter inequity exists but it is generally believed that it does, and certainly suspicion is justified by the fact that sugar and salt in small quantities and at high prices can be bought in the camp. Does this stuff come in 'over the wire', i.e. from the black market or trade with natives or Korean guards, or does it come from the cookhouse? Who can say?

Then there are those who become rich in dollars; some fabulously rich, either by selling their property, rings, watches, certain articles of clothing, etc., to the Korean guards, or through their agents in Singapore City, or by acting as agents in the camp for those POWs who had property which they wished to convert into dollars, the agents, of course, getting a good commission, possibly a secret commission on top of the usual percentage commission and so doubling their profit.

It was possible, also, to acquire dollars in large amounts by writing a cheque or a promissory note in favour of one of these camp capitalists, the cheque or promissory note being in pounds and payable after the war. Some of the capitalists developed such an avaricious eye to the future that they demanded one pound for every five, three or even two dollars Japanese. When one considers the level at which canteen prices stood at that time, e.g. $32 for a pound of dried white bait, $12 for a pound of tapioca flour, $20 for a pound of blachang (stinking prawn paste), one must rate these transactions as not only heartless but also unworthy of that comradeship which should exist in the Services — sheer unabashed, daylight robbery. Those with capital eat extras with meals and between meals, and often in large amounts, and often without any apparent thought of the many who were without means and property to sell. Most of the latter class were men who had been up-country in 1943 and who had come back at the end of that year or early in the next bereft of everything including sufficiency of clothing or footwear.

There was much individual kindness and help given to the unfortunate and the bedridden but, on the whole, a spirit was developing in the camp that was selfish and unchristian in a concern for one's own food and one's own welfare which occupied too great a part of the day's duties and an unconcern for sickness, suffering and death.

Amongst some medical officers, the tendency was to become philosophical about the latter state of affairs as it applied to others and to regard it as inevitable. With other people, the tendency was to keep out of the wards, or, at any rate, not to look too much.

Another factor which militated against the distress was the general knowledge that amongst the wealthiest people were a few private soldiers, or soldiers of low military rank, especially the astute traders and agents mentioned above and, in consequence of this, it was not uncommon to hear the remark made that the other ranks had more money than the officers. It was a popular form of self-justification amongst the more selfish of the officers and an attitude that tended to handicap or even to bring into derision the time-honoured principle of noblesse oblige.

It distressed some of the officers, myself included, to see some men, even if only a few, starving and penniless whilst others throve and grew fat on what they were able to purchase at the canteen. Not that the latter were living luxuriously, far from it, because at the canteen one could only buy food such as whitebait, blachang, tapioca flour, a small and unsavoury choice! But still *food*. And the first and last items I mention could even be made tasty. In fact, the cakes, biscuits, pancakes, etc., concocted from tapioca flour, palm oil, salt and some flavouring such as blachang, garlic or sage from the garden, were legion in variety and protein in form. The cooking of such 'leggies' as they were called, as well as various kinds of whitebait and vegetable pasties and stews, went on by day and by night both in the officers' kitchen and at the little brazier and mud oven fires made by the men around their huts. The Commanding Officer was wise and liberal in allowing the men to have these fires and fuel for them, the only proviso being that the fires must not be in dangerous positions, such as underneath huts.

The group of officers, concerned for the very poorest men, conferred together to see if anything could be done by way of voluntary contribution to help those so much less fortunate, starting, initially, amongst the officers.

Note: By way of explanation, in the Selarang and POW area, different army units, e.g. infantry battalions or their remnants, and gunners, service corps, engineers, etc. were housed in different buildings, scattered over, say, a square mile of country, in part flat and in part divided by slopes and watercourses or deep concrete drains. Each group had a letter designating it, e.g. A Group, B Group, C Group, etc. and was divided, at least as far as the larger groups were concerned, into houses with numbers, e.g. house 216, house 148, etc. Most groups had their own chicken runs or duck yards.

At the hospital, we had many duck yards, yards belonging to groups of individuals such as three or four officers in a combine, or a group of a similar number of NCOs and a few belonged to groups of private soldiers. As well as these, there was a large yard containing about 80 birds belonging to the hospital personnel as a whole, and another communal yard with about 40 ducks belonging to the Officers' Mess as a whole.

Extract From a Letter Written From Kranji, Dated 30 August 1945, to his Wife

This letter was never posted but it was found among other papers with the diary.
These last three weeks (all but two days) have been a dream of delight thinking all the while of seeing you again — and our darling children. Thank God for Peace again, and for Victory for our cause.

I have been, like you, so much in the dark wondering, during the months between letters, how you all were and what was happening, and thinking, too, of your anxiety about me. I don't know yet how this letter will go, or when, but I am getting it written and ready for the arrival of our people and, as I hope an air-mail will soon be established, I will not make it a long letter.

Since the Japanese surrender, which we heard about by our secret camp wireless set, we have been on tenterhooks and listening breathlessly to each day's bulletin passed round between us. Then, at last, about ten days ago, the Japanese guard-sergeant came out with the news to us officially so there was no longer need for secrecy. Since that day, they have not ceased to lavish food and Red Cross parcels on us.

After months, if not years, of actual starvation, the patients in these huts are now actually getting sick from over-eating and from over-smoking, too, for the Japanese ply us with cigars and cheroots and cigarettes more than we can smoke.

I am thin but very well. My last letters were three from you all received here on the same date — 24 July 1945, but written on different dates, viz: Southport, 6 September, Armidale, 13 September, and Armidale, 31 October 1944. Before that, none for many months.

For many families, alas! the light of life will seem to have gone out when the lists from this country reach Australia and England, and India, too. Thousands of Indians, as well as our men, must have died up in Burma and Siam on that accursed railway which the Japanese built with our labour — from near Bangkok to Moulmein. That is where most of our losses occurred from disease and starvation and overwork.

I was spared that ordeal and was left the whole time with those who remained at or near Changi on Singapore Island. Then, a year ago, some of us were sent to this hut camp about 20 miles from Changi.

I have been kept fairly busy all through with our sick men, mostly relics from the North. It has been a blessing to have work to do.

A trailer party bringing wood to the Krangji hospital

The Changi area, looking south-east

George McNeilly, organiser of many musical functions at Changi

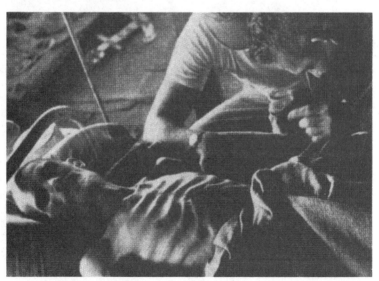

A prisoner-of-war patient, starved and overworked by the Japanese

TO ALL ALLIED PRISONERS OF WAR

THE JAPANESE FORCES HAVE SURRENDERED UNCONDITIONALLY AND THE WAR IS OVER

WE will get supplies to you as soon as is humanly possible and will make arrangements to get you out but, owing to the distances involved, it may be some time before we can achieve this.

YOU will help us and yourselves if you act as follows :—

(1) Stay in your camp until you get further orders from us.

(2) Start preparing nominal rolls of personnel, giving fullest particulars.

(3) List your most urgent necessities.

(4) If you have been starved or underfed for long periods DO NOT eat large quantities of solid food, fruit or vegetables at first. It is dangerous for you to do so. Small quantities at frequent intervals are much safer and will strengthen you far more quickly. For those who are really ill or very weak, fluids such as broth and soup, making use of the water in which rice and other foods have been boiled, are much the best. Gifts of food from the local population should be cooked. We want to get you back home quickly, safe and sound, and we do not want to risk your chances from diarrhoea, dysentry and cholera at this last stage.

(5) Local authorities and/or Allied officers will take charge of your affairs in a very short time. Be guided by their advice.

On 28 August 1945 this leaflet was dropped over Changi. On the back were instructions to the Japanese on how to treat prisoners

A great welcome home for one of
Dr Huxtable's patients

Dr Huxtable, a flying
doctor after World War II,
on the way to an emergency
case at Caradoc station

An outback mother thanks Dr Huxtable for his help in saving her
child during his service with the Flying Doctor service

165

Index